The Black Family's Guide to Healing Emotional Wounds

The Black Family's Guide to Healing Emotional Wounds

Nijiama Smalls
and
Shamon Smalls

Nvision Global

All scripture quotations are from the Holy Bible New
International Version, 2011.

ISBN:
HARDCOVER - 978-1-7346928-8-4
PAPERBACK - 978-1-7346928-7-7
EBOOK - 978-1-7346928-9-1

Library Of Congress
Names: Smalls, Nijiama
Contributor: Smalls, Shamon

Identifier: Library of Congress Control Number: 2024932937

Dedicated to all of those who, like us, aim to make sense of the past and are ready to thrive.

Contents

∞

Prologue

How to Read This Book

The words in this book do not come lightly. Each concept comes from the culmination of over three years of devoted research, case study reviews, and data collection. Our lived experiences have also been documented for additional context.

The focus of this work isn't to portray Black America as small, monolithic, or victims, but to trace the roots of our pain to deliver a clear understanding that leads to healing. Our primary objective is for Black America individually and collectively to heal the pain points in our lives that steal our joy and compromise our success.

Told by Nijiama with insights and contributions by Shamon, the key ideas of this work are supported by cultural and historical context. We are taking readers of this book on a journey of the heart and soul. From beginning to end, prepare to be challenged, inspired, and humored as we guide you through a journey of self-awareness and healing.

The introduction serves as a mirror to help us see ourselves and how we show up which leads into the technical aspects of our trauma. Each chapter afterward, the soul of this book, covers an emotional wound that we have found to be common amongst Black American families, through research. We provide specific examples for clarity and illustration.

The majority of us on this planet arrive here through some form of relationship between a man and woman regardless of how temporary or whole that relationship may be. And that is one of the first relationships we are acquainted with as children. For this reason, many anecdotes from our marriage are intertwined because the way we showed up in our home was a product of how we were parented. It also has a tremendous impact on how we parent our children and the adults they will choose to become – this perspective leads us to the needed work of addressing and overcoming generational trauma.

The final section of this book provides a path to healing —the way forward. Each step is actionable and can be implemented immediately.

Note that not every part of this book will resonate with you. We encourage you to glean what you need and use those tools to guide you through the steps to heal.

You may read this alone or in a group, however, spend as much time as you can sitting with each chapter allowing yourself to accept your feelings. Don't rush it – healing requires time and patience. Marinate on the text as well as your thoughts and feelings regarding each wound.

The questions at the end of each chapter are hard; they go beyond the surface and you may find this uncomfortable initially. You may also find that overall this isn't an easy read as it may trigger painful memories and require you to sit with emotions and feelings you have buried. Please see a therapist if this becomes too overwhelming for you. Understand that this trek is painful at times but worth it because the inner peace and new perspective you will gain is unsurpassable. This is deeply spiritual and soul work and its impact is life-changing and mindset-shifting– and not to be misprized.

Grab your journals and let's dig in.

The Browns

The great-grandchildren of freed slaves from York County, South Carolina, Mr. and Mrs. Brown built a home and raised their six daughters in the Bible belt. Except for the two oldest, the daughters still live in the home that was built by Mr. and Mrs. Brown with their children. They remain in the home partially out of fear and also out of convenience. Today they are a very close-knit family. Yet, poverty, toxic relationships, and mental health issues have plagued their lives.

Over the years, the family began to notice changes regarding the behavior of one of the youngest siblings, Karen. As she entered her late twenties and after the death of her father, Karen began to complain of hearing voices and feared that federal agents were following her. This continued for some time. The family tried to ignore it, hoping it would go away – it didn't. It just grew worse as the years progressed.

Eventually, the voices Karen heard interfered with her daily life and made it difficult for her to maintain employment because her colleagues found her behavior disruptive and, in some instances, frightening. So she was encouraged to resign. Being unable to provide for herself and her only daughter Sabrina, the family stepped in to help. They moved them into what is now known as the family home and handled their financial affairs.

As the years progressed, Karen's behavior continued to change drastically, and soon the community began to take notice. They received calls from neighbors stating that Karen was found dancing in the middle of the park during the day, at the grocery store arguing out loud with herself, and roaming the streets in the middle of the night barely clothed. The family found Karen's behavior uncontrollable and embarrassing.

Karen was eventually arrested for making a violent threat via telephone to a US government official. As a consequence, she was remanded to treatment at a state mental health hospital where she was diagnosed with psychosis. There she was fed a heavy dosage of drugs that left her overly sedated, numb, and drowsy. The family considered their options as they tried to decide what to do with her upon her release. Keeping her locked in a bedroom in the house so she would not cause harm to others or embarrass the family appeared to be the best option. On the occasions that she refused to take her meds and her behavior became too erratic, they would have her detained for weeks at a time in a state-operated hospital miles away from home.

For Sabrina, her younger years were a challenge. Her mother became the laughingstock of the neighborhood as her peers made jokes mocking her mother's odd behavior. Over time, Sabrina began to experience shame when anyone mentioned her mother.

Although Sabrina was surrounded by support from her family, she often felt a sense of loss and neglect by not having a mentally-well mother in her life.

There were times when her aunts would place the needs of their children above hers which often left her feeling unseen as if her needs were not urgent. Because of this, there were many instances in which she did not receive dental treatment and healthcare when it was needed. She also found herself wearing tattered underwear because she didn't have money to replace them.

Sabrina longed for a relationship with her mother; the kind the other girls her age had with their mothers. Because Karen was unable to fill that for Sabrina, it left her with a void. She never addressed it with the family, instead, she internalized it by pouring over the thoughts for hours throughout the day locking it all inside of her emotions.

Sabrina didn't want to cause any additional troubles for her family so she focused on being a good student. She earned good grades and scholarships to college. After finishing high school, she attended college and earned her degree.

Later, Sabrina found a position at a small accounting firm that matched her personality as she discovered herself to be more of an introvert preferring books and films over people interaction. She found it easy to take things personally and conflict with people overwhelmed her.

Her family were church-going people who were committed to prayer so for a time that tended to be a haven for Sabrina and where she was able to find community. However, after a disagreement with one of the lay members she became discouraged from attending church. It was during this time that she also began to question– if God was as good as they claimed, why was she born to a mentally ill mother? Why did some of her needs go unmet? It just didn't seem to work for her the way the church claimed. Because of her grievances with God, she decided to leave the church altogether.

Eventually, she met a guy, Ian, who she began to date. He introduced her to the teachings of the Black Hebrew Israelites. Initially, she found it appealing as it helped to explain the history of Black Americans and their origins. She spent quite a bit of time listening, with him to the teachings, but she found it too restrictive, rigid, and irate. During this time her anxiety began to increase and migraines began appearing.

After the relationship with Ian ended, she began practicing the Yoruba religion and worshiping Olodumare. This religion resonated with her because it made her feel close and connected to her deceased ancestors whom she deeply admired, particularly the ones who loved her deeply —especially, the now-deceased Mr. and Mrs. Brown. She also believed it helped to explain her life of pain. She now deems herself a healer who must overcome adversity to help others however she still feels an empty void.

As time went on, Sabrina discovered her battle with mental health. She noticed that she was very sensitive to certain conversations and emotions. She noticed that those hurts would have tremendous power over her to the point that she distanced herself from some of her family members who truly cared for her. She also became easily agitated, impulsive, and at other times saddened to the point of being suicidal.

Jared and Lauren

Getting out of his silver, six-series BMW, thirty-year-old Jared is amongst the highest-earning employees at one of the largest defense consulting firms in Washington, DC. Armed with a Master's degree in Cyber Security, Jared has earned many certifications which has helped him to quickly ascend to the top of the corporate ladder.

He walks into the office building with his head held high but low enough to take note of those who glance towards him. "Nice suit," says the receptionist as she notices the firmly fitted trendy suit that Jared is wearing. As he walks towards his office, Jared stops by the interns' office to share the details of his weekend trip to Miami with an Instagram model named Meghan. This has become a part of his daily routine as the interns are forced to listen to the details that he shares about his many dates, his new condo in a luxury high-rise building across the street from the Tyson's Center mall in McLean, VA, and his new toy of the month which is usually a new car or motorcycle.

After a weekend filled with dates, hook-ups, and time with his grad school peers, Jared winds down by spending Sundays with family at his parent's home. Jared's mother (a retired school teacher) and father (a manufacturing manager) live about an hour away in Owings Mills, MD. Jared looks forward to the home-cooked meals his mom prepares on Sundays and their weekly talks. He also looks forward to catching up with his younger sister, Lauren.

Lauren is a nurse who looks up to her older brother. She and her mom are proud of him and adore him. They both watched him transform himself from a short, awkward, bullied teen to a handsome well-educated muscular man with a thriving career.

Growing up, their mother was a very hands-on parent. She attended all of their school events, helped with homework, took them to church, and birthday parties, and arranged play dates. They both talk to her quite heavily during the week and look to her for advice and guidance on life issues.

The relationship between the two siblings and their father, on the other hand, isn't as solid. Their father, a gruff man, who focused much of his time on being the family provider rarely spent time tending to the emotional needs of his children. Growing up, both Jared and Lauren found him to be cold, distant, and critical. There weren't many hugs or kisses distributed from him and he always seemed to be grouchy or in a bad mood.

Jared feared and even loathed their father at times because of his tough discipline. Lauren found him to be strict and very rigid so she kept him out of the loop and rarely went to him for guidance.

On Sundays, during their visits there is limited interaction with their father. Typically, the family patriarch can be found watching sports in a separate room while drinking a cold beer – hoping to not be disturbed.

Quentin

Spending weekends at his grandmother's house was a special time for ten-year-old Quentin. His grandmother would make huge meals while the grandchildren played in the yard until night, catching lightning bugs (aka fireflies) and frogs with mason jars.

One evening, while playing hide and seek with his cousins, Quentin scurried to hide behind a pile of bushes on the side of the house. The bushes were tall, green, and thick so for him, this created a perfect hiding spot. As he remained there, one of his older cousins, Gwen, joined him in the hideout. He welcomed her – reminding her to remain quiet so they would not be discovered.

As they patiently waited with the hopes of not being discovered, he felt Gwen's hands glide down his torso and then make their way to his groin. Quentin was surprised. This had never happened to him before. So initially, he was unsure of what was happening. She unbuttoned his pants and placed her hand inside. It felt weird and awkward, scary even but he was too afraid to tell her to stop. He froze and stood silently. He pretended not to notice hoping it would stop – but she continued. Finally, he heard his cousin scream the words, "Got you!" Those words brought a sense of relief to Quentin as he ran out of the bushes.

Later, as his mother came to pick him up, Gwen whispered to him, "Don't tell."

Quentin wrestled with making sense of the incident. When he was alone, he cried about it because it felt so wrong and awkward. Eventually, he decided to put it out of his mind, choosing to pretend it never happened.

As Quentin grew older, he became a bit more curious about the opposite sex. Although his experience with Gwen felt awkward, he began to acknowledge that a portion of that moment felt good to him. This singular incident awakened a desire inside him that he couldn't quite place and it made him want more. He found himself daydreaming while gazing at women on television imagining them naked touching their private parts. Whether it was a music video filled with scantily clad, underdressed women with big booties and firm tits; or movies showing couples making love it caught his attention.

What fueled it, even more, were the comments made by friends and family members – "Quentin, you are such a cutie, how many girlfriends do you have?" He was also privy to conversations in which he heard his father and uncles discuss various women such as the new girlfriend of the month or the women they were interested in while celebrating whom they conquered. During these conversations, they would turn to young Quentin to ask, "Boy, have you knocked down any yet? I know you are still not a virgin."

As Quentin moved into his teenage years, he grew handsome and became an athlete. By the time Quentin was nineteen years old, he had been involved in numerous romantic relationships. These relationships would start great yet fizzle primarily due to miscommunication or his loss of interest. It almost always led to his infidelity in some form. By Quentin's twenty-third birthday, he had fathered three children by three different young women and was dating a completely different woman. With very limited education and work experience, he found it hard to care for the families he created which kept him at odds with his children's mothers. This eventually led him to legal trouble.

Quentin became filled with resentment towards all of the stress that he was under. He found life to be overwhelming and draining making it difficult for him to get out of bed on some days. He turned to marijuana and heavy drinking to numb the pain.

Charlotte

She stormed through the front door of the house slamming it so hard it shook the table and shattered the mirror above it. Charlotte, born and raised in Newark by a single mother, didn't take a look back to notice the damage done by her door slam. Mark, Charlotte's husband, looked up from the stove as he was stirring the meatballs for dinner. Immediately, he saw her tears noticing she was deeply upset.

"Bae, are you ok?"

"No, I'm not," Charlotte said as she threw her bag onto the floor.

"What happened?" replied Mark.

"It was the meeting at Liam's school. It was terrible! Those idiots don't know what they are talking about or who they are messing with! They are trying to say that something is wrong with our son. So I cursed them out and walked out."

"What do you mean, Charlotte?"

"They said Liam is falling behind in his work and has a hard time keeping up with the lessons. They want us to get him tested. I'm not doing no shit like that!"

"Tested for what?" inquired Mark.

"They are saying he may have some developmental delays. I screamed at those teachers and cursed them out!" she stated proudly.

"Oh God, no!" Mark placed his face in the palm of his hands. "Well, let's calm down."

Charlotte's rage intensified as she replied, "No, I'm not calming down! They are saying that something is wrong with our child! After this, I'm sure that they will try to kick him out and put him in a different school. I'm not going to allow that to happen."

"I think we need to hear them out. According to the note they sent they just want to get him extra support to help him keep up." Mark replied

"What do you mean? This is our son we are talking about! We will not hear them out! They will put him on a bunch of drugs to alter his mind and kick him out of school. I'm not going to allow that!"

"I think you may be overreacting. Why don't you reach out to the school counselor that you are friends with? She may be able to shed some light."

"I don't speak to her anymore."

"Why not?"

"Because she didn't respond to the invitation I sent her for my Valentine's Day event."

"Perhaps she was busy," Mark said as he shrugged.

"No, I'm sure she just blew it off because she thinks she is better than me. I cursed her out about it and told her not to say another word to me."

"I'm going to start going to that school every single day just in case they try to harm him or convince him something is wrong with him. I need to be able to explain what happens to him if they do harm him. I also want to get him switched to another teacher. I don't want Mrs. Jackson around my son anymore if she believes something is wrong with him."

Mark aimed to calm her down, "I don't know if that's a good idea. I'm Liam's dad and I want to know what she saw in him to make her conclude that he needs to be tested."

"Listen! I called Aileen and told her about it on the ride home. She agreed with me – one hundred percent."

Mark looked over his shoulder and replied, "Should we be taking advice from your best friend? She doesn't have any children! Besides, she was recently fired from her job and she gambles away all of her money each month. Not a good person to take advice from, if you ask me."

"So! She is still my best friend and sees things the way I do."

Mark responded, "I have an idea. Our neighbor who is always at the bus stop with her son. She serves on the PTO. Let's talk to her about this."

"No, I don't like her either because she commented that she thinks her daughter is too young to get her hair braided. I think she was throwing shade at me for braiding Kya's hair. I can't remember her exact words but I never want to see her again."

In frustration and all out of ideas to help his son yet wanting to keep the peace with his wife, Mark sighed. Later that evening, a letter arrived addressed to Charlotte hand delivered by a messenger. The letter read in a nutshell, "For the safety of our staff, due to your threats and unprofessional candor, we ask that you do not return to our school."

Nijiama

It was on a warm and beautiful day in early August that Shamon and I got married at a quaint country club in Laurel, Maryland. Our friends and family traveled from near and far to celebrate our union. To say we were excited would be an understatement as we had spent over a year researching, planning, and organizing down to the smallest detail for our wedding day – the day I had dreamed about since childhood, the day I sometimes felt would never come. But in all the planning, the one thing we did not anticipate was that the unhealed emotional wounds that we both kept buried would rise to the surface as soon as we left for the honeymoon.

I wish I could tell you that the first few years of our marriage were filled with champagne, laughter, strawberries, and sunshine. Frankly, it was quite the opposite. The first two years of marriage for Shamon and I was the toughest. Our finances were tight, we lived in a very tiny apartment, and we fought about everything! We fought about how to manage our finances, how and when meals should be prepared, how to spend our time, and every off-beat action was taken as an offense. Not only did we fight but we fought hard. Whew chile! And it was how we fought that made things the most difficult. Unfortunately, I subconsciously unleashed the pain I held inside from my childhood onto him. It was the pain from believing my mother didn't love me that I never dealt with. Therefore, like a maniac, I yelled, cursed, belittled him, and screamed to make my point. Shamon, on the other hand, raised his voice and put his fist through walls to make his point. At other times, he shut down and made silence his weapon of choice. Just toxic y'all. On the outside, however, no one had the slightest idea.

Unresolved pain not only resurfaced during the first years of our marriage, but it pulled up to the dinner table and took a seat impacting every single area of our relationship. It's interesting how we tend to project the hurts we gain from others onto the people closest to us, the ones who love us the most, the ones who do the most for us. You see, the issue for us was that we were unaware of the hurts that still dwelt inside of us, the trauma that ran through our veins that was passed down from our ancestors, the resentment from past hurts that were never resolved, and the destructive behavior we kept hidden while we dated. Sure some of that surfaced while we were dating but we ignored it, to be quite honest with you. Our priority was getting married because for us marriage meant the start of success and stability. It was the life we both envisioned for ourselves and nothing was going to get in the way of that. We both ignored the red flags and proceeded. But once we said I do, split the bills, removed the masks, and settled in, it all rose to the surface. As we would later discover, the problems that arose in our marriage did not begin on the day we got married. Many of those issues began way before we were born.

This was a time when I believe I was at my worst and it impacted every area of my life. Like landmines waiting for someone to say or do something to set them off, my heart was filled with many unhealed emotional wounds. If a colleague or professional associate did something that annoyed me, I made it an offense and held on to it. And I had to let them know about it in the most confrontational way possible, every single time. I was hypercritical of others and gossip was my ammunition and means to bond and build relationships. I was cold and unwelcoming of anyone I didn't know. Any new projects I was put on at work I'd find a way to be negative about it or criticize it to death eventually pulling others into my torment. I fully embraced being difficult because somehow I believed it gave me power.

What helped to improve us and our marriage was healing. We had to do the hard work – the spiritual and soul work, to heal the inner chaos. It required both of us to dig deep into our history to discover where our pain stemmed from and develop enough discipline to regulate ourselves. This was important to us because having a whole marriage was more important than holding on to our past hurts and toxic behavior. Moreover, we wanted to create a family unit that was whole and different from what we both were privy to as children.

Shamon

As Nij mentioned she believed she was at her worst during this time, for me I believe I was at my lowest in terms of maturity. Before Nij, I only experienced casual relationships with women. The relationship with Nij, however, required a lot of me; more of my time, attention, accountability, and communication. Things that I had been able to get away with in my previous relationships, Nij just wasn't entertaining. That, of course, caused some friction.

Additionally, I am non-confrontational by nature, so I don't engage in back-and-forth arguing as I find it draining and a waste of my time. It's just not how I'm wired whereas that seemed to be Nij's wheelhouse. She can debate about almost any topic endlessly beating it to death!

To add to all of this, coming from a home of divorced parents, I didn't understand my role of being protector and priest to Nij. I did not understand how to protect her heart and to be the priest of her soul. This required emotional maturity, self-control, and awareness on my behalf that had not been modeled before me. I had to learn to communicate openly with her and study her so that she and I could remain in tune.

Being raised in a family, we gain tools that will either become helpful or harmful to us. For example, we may learn healthy ways to handle conflict, and

gain self-confidence. Other tools we gain can be those
we pick up to survive in our family such as lying,
lust, hustling, anxieties, manipulation, and anger.
These tools impact all of our relationships including
marriage. Because I grew up experiencing quite a bit
of financial challenges, I became a minimizer. So I
would often say to Nij when her feelings were hurt;
"It's not that deep."
"I can't believe you are upset about something so
trivial."

In my mind, I believed this was the correct answer
to give her because for me nothing was as severe as
being a child facing food insecurities as was the case
for me growing up. However, I had to understand the
importance of validating her feelings and making her
feel seen.

And let us assure you that as Believers, we both
had premarital counseling. It certainly provided us
with tools and resources but we needed counseling
that took us on a deep dive and addressed our
unhealed emotional wounds while providing us with a
fundamental understanding of what marriage required
of us. You see, many people believe that the first few
years of marriage are the best – usually called 'the
honeymoon phase'. That's incorrect! The first years
are typically the toughest because achieving oneness
is not easy. It's similar to attempting to mesh two
metal components together. In order, to do so there
will be some friction, sharpening, and molding; and
that makes for lots of discomfort. To say we were ill-
prepared was an understatement.

I believe there is a moment in marriage where you begin to feel a bit shackled so to speak. It hits you that you are now accountable to another person, you have to consider them, share schedules, discuss peeves and annoyances healthily, you have to discuss major purchases, you compromise on daily dinner plans, and they may find some of the platonic friendships that you once had with other women to be uncomfortable for them. Although you may be aware of this before marriage when it hits you that this is the way it is, it can be a bit of a shock. So to survive we had to heal. I'm grateful that seventeen years later, we not only survived but are thriving.

While doing the work, we began to notice patterns. The inner chaos we experienced not only impacted our marriage, but in various shapes and forms, it also made an impact on all of our relationships both personally and professionally. Therefore, healing not only drastically improved our marriage but also improved every relationship around us. We are better parents, leaders, siblings, colleagues, friends, mentors, and neighbors all because of healing. We are also kinder to ourselves and one another because of healing as well. As a bonus to our healing, what also improved was our relationships with our finances and time.

We first had to begin by asking ourselves a very hard question – what happened to us? As we began to seek the answer we realized that it wasn't simply about what happened to us, but the story we told ourselves about what happened to us. You see, quite like the families in the introduction, the story we tell ourselves determines how we show up in this world.

It determines if we see ourselves as conquerors, victors, and overcomers or merely hopeless victims. It determines if we see ourselves as free to give and receive love, or eerily guarded and easily triggered.

Now, let us assure you that this book isn't about marriage, for the most part, but about all familial relationships in general. This book is about how unhealed trauma can impact those relationships, particularly the relationships we have with ourselves. You see, if we continue to sabotage our external relationships we are ultimately sabotaging ourselves, our opportunities (like the individuals and families in the introduction), and ultimately our inner peace. People are vehicles for us that land us to various destinations. So when we sabotage our relationships with others, we are destroying not only our inner peace but our personal and/or professional opportunities. Every opportunity we will obtain will come through a person. Our net worth is truly tied to our network. How we manage and deal with other people is critical.

This book isn't about blame but the contrary. It's about understanding where our wounds stem. It's also about challenging our perspectives, many of those we gained during our most painful moments, to understand how we view the world. Often our self-destruction is due to our perspective. When we have not healed, we often view life through the lens of our unhealed emotional wounds.

Particularly for Black Americans, because our existence within this country has been traumatic at best, and to this day we still suffer internally. We have had to fight just to enjoy basic freedoms that every human should be entitled to and so today, many of us still view life out of "the fight". When someone offends us, we fight; when we take something personally, we fight; when we are aggravated, we fight. These are the behaviors that were birthed out of our most desperate times that may not be necessarily helpful to us today. It robs us of our peace and joy. We have a legacy of emotional trauma that we continue to transfer through our generations that impacts how we show up in this world.

It is time for our community to do some unpacking of our trauma so that we can look at how we are showing up. We all know that we have some toxic behaviors but until we deal with the root causes, we can never be whole. The dysfunction that shows up in our families, the way that we handle our offenses and what we choose to take offense to, the way that we rear our children, our relationship with finances, our feelings towards faith, as well as the destructive choices we make, are all factors pointing us to wounds that must be addressed and healed.

This book is intended for every member of the family, regardless of gender, whether you are married or not, whether you have children or not, and whether you have a job or not. Regardless of your role and position in life, it is time for us, as a community, to heal.

For our internal peace, it's imperative that we heal!

For our future generations, it's imperative that we heal!

So that we can realize our opportunities, it's imperative that we heal!

So that we can continue to shatter glass ceilings, it's imperative that we heal!

So that we can unite and become a solid community, it's imperative that we heal!

Questions for Reflection:

1. Which of the characters in the introduction do see commonalities?

2. What areas in your life do you believe self-sabotage has played a part?

3. What toxic behavior do you believe you bring to your relationships?

Chapter 1

Unhealed Emotional Wounds

"Unhealed emotional wounds steal from us—they take away our happiness, joy, and peace."

— **Nijiama Smalls,** *The Black Girl's Guide to Healing Emotional Wounds*

Nijiama

I once had a colleague who injured his thumb by slamming it into a car door. Assuming it was a minor injury, he simply bandaged it and took some pain meds hoping that it would heal on its own. Over time, his thumb began to experience intense pain when it was grazed even in the slightest. Suddenly, it began to turn green. The doctor told him that the thumb had not healed properly from the injury and was now infected. Unhealed emotional wounds are very similar to physical wounds. Both, if not healed properly, once they are poked, prodded, or triggered will cause us to feel pain whether it's physical or emotional – feeling the pain causes us to react.

Our painful past experiences change us. When we do not heal, we allow our worst moments to define and shape us. We lose our ability to see the good in situations and people, enjoy the simple moments, persevere through conflict, and bring our best selves to our relationships. Unhealed emotional wounds will completely disrupt our lives causing us to be callous with the feelings of others and do things that are harmful to our emotions.

Unhealed emotional wounds are painful past experiences that we never processed properly or genuinely dealt with in a way that brings us to healing. Often when painful situations occur, we bury them in our subconscious believing that if we do not think about them they will not harm us. For us, it often feels less painful if we don't have to think or talk about it. This is the incorrect way to manage pain because if we don't deal with our hurts, they resurface in our relationships and wreak havoc causing us to harm the people who are closest to us. It may sound crazy but the saying is true that we hurt the ones who love us the most.

When my children were younger, their hearts were always filled with love and excitement. They sometimes cried when we disciplined them or when they did not get their way but within a few minutes, they'd bounced back to their old selves, completely over it and excited about the next thing. The simplest things such as seeing butterflies or a rainbow filled them with so much joy. Going for a walk in the park was a pleasure for them. Giving them a few bucks for a cone of ice cream was a treat that topped off their day. If a friend took their toy, there was anger and frustration and maybe even a spat between the two but minutes later the spat was over and they'd return to playing together as if it never happened. I believe that this behavior is truly the best version of ourselves. This is how we handle life before we ever meet pain, loss, and suffering. This is what Jesus means in the Bible when He encourages us to be like children. But life happens and all that comes along with it – toxic relationships, divorce, betrayals, abuse, assault, disappointments, death, illness, rejection, financial setbacks, shattered dreams, etc. – emotional wounds. If left unhealed these chip away at our self-worth and joy.

I can recall disagreeing with a friend. She did something that I found off-putting. For some reason, I could not let it go. I replayed the situation in my mind which made it about me and it became a part of me. I began to feel as if I was going to explode with anger if I did not address it with her. We decided to meet to discuss our issues. During the discussion, I was far from agreeable and was not interested in understanding what she had to say or gaining a sense of her perspective. I aimed to get everything I was thinking and feeling out on the table. To me, it felt good to get things off of my chest and to believe I was being heard. However, this severely damaged my relationship with a person who had shown me an abundance of kindness.

Believing that my feelings were bottled up triggered me causing emotional stress. Through lots of therapy (thank God for therapy) I discovered that this is because as a child there were many times I didn't feel understood and I didn't feel as though I had a voice. What I have learned is that behavior that doesn't align with peace and joy is usually rooted in immaturity, chemical imbalances, hormonal differences, or unhealed emotional wounds.

When we are triggered, it is because the incident or situation has activated a place inside of us that has not healed. For this reason, we must understand our triggers and where they derive from as we will discuss later in this book. Our quality of life is centered around the decisions that we make. We sabotage ourselves when we react poorly when we are triggered or make decisions out of our unhealed emotions. Therefore, we need to understand the following:

The way we react toward our boss or leader is not always about them; it's about our childhood wounds, particularly the wounds we carry from the way we were parented.

-When we fight with our ex, we may be projecting our hurts from past rejection, abandonment, and unresolved conflict.

-When someone says something that we take personally and hold onto it's pointing us towards the unhealed places inside of us that we have not addressed.

-Lashing out at someone who does something off-putting to us can signal how we feel about being in uncomfortable or unwanted situations.

-The arguments with our parents and siblings could be about the acceptance we perhaps didn't feel in our family as a child.

-The disagreements and lack of trust we have for our romantic partner could be the past betrayals from previous relationships resurfacing and wreaking havoc.

This is what is meant by being triggered.
Please understand that being triggered is not necessarily a bad thing. What can be bad is responding negatively or unhealthily to the triggers. We must learn to embrace our triggers because they

are telling us that we have unhealed wounds that require our attention.

So it was during our marriage that we both experienced triggers from unhealed emotional wounds that we didn't know how to handle. These wounds were tearing us apart and exploding in our faces. The late-night arguments, the days we spent not speaking to each other, the enmity we held that we kept throwing in each other's faces to use as ammunition were all because we were triggered by the unhealed emotional wounds inside of us and the toxic learned behavior we had adopted. This is all very natural because relationships make us close and the closer we become to a person the more of our flaws and traumas they will see.

On one evening, we sat down together and had one of the most difficult conversations of my life. It was the night that Shamon told me how difficult my outbursts were for him to handle and I shared how his silence was harmful to me. We realized then that if we both didn't make changes we weren't going to last and we would carry on the tradition of raising children in a broken environment. That conversation began our process of healing and I'm very grateful for it. We are now free to love from the best parts of ourselves without our past pain interfering. The joy in our home and the emotional peace we now experience is priceless! And it can be the same for you.

Question for Reflection

Describe a situation in which you were triggered and reacted poorly. How could you have handled the situation differently?

Chapter 2

Transgenerational Trauma

*"Marginalized peoples—excluded, minimized, shamed—
are traumatized peoples, because as we've discussed,
humans are fundamentally relational creatures. To be
excluded or dehumanized in an organization, community,
or society you are part of results in prolonged,
uncontrollable stress that is sensitizing."*
— Oprah Winfrey, *What Happened To You?:*
Conversations on Trauma, Resilience, and Healing

Nijiama

In the hit Netflix stand-up special *Selective Outrage*, Chris Rock shared a story about his mother who was born in a town in South Carolina during the 1940s. In this town, like many others during this time, if a Black person could not find a Black dentist, White dentists refused to serve them. Therefore, his mother and many others were forced to receive dental work from a veterinarian. The same instruments that were used to pull the teeth of horses and other farm animals were used to extract his mother's teeth.[1] What a shame. This is systematic oppression and it has the power to change the DNA of the oppressed for generations to come– transgenerational trauma.[2]

From reconstruction through the 1960s, many cities in the South as well as the town of Rock Hill, SC, where I was raised were under submission to an awful monster referred to as Jim Crow. These statutes that were upheld by Plessy vs Ferguson dehumanized dark skin and discouraged racial mingling. When racial intermingling was necessary, Jim Crow made sure to keep Black Americans in a place of utter inferiority by forcing us to sit in the back of buses, enter through back doors, or be served inferior meals at public restaurants only after white families feasted on the best.[3]

At this time, public schools were segregated until the mid-60s when forced integration occurred. For a time, this did not solve the problem– only exasperated it. My mother vividly can recall being taught by educators who were raised to hate dark skin and they did very little to hide their disdain for our race. By being standoffish, exclusive, vile, and blatantly racist, White students and administrators made it known to my mother and the other Black students that their presence was unwelcome.[4] I can't imagine a child being treated so harshly by people who were supposed to ensure their safety and future. Today, we have many anti-bullying campaigns dedicated to protecting our children. What happens when a child is reared in an environment in which the educators, administrators, and leaders are the bullies?

During this time, in many parts of the US, white families began leaving the cities to move to the suburbs known as white flight to remain distant from Black America.[5] For example, real-estate writer and researcher Jon Gorey states, "In 1950, Chicago was 86% white, with more than 3 million white residents. By 1980, the city's Black population had more than doubled, from about 492,000 to 1.2 million. At the same time, more than 1.5 million white Chicagoans had moved out."[6]

Because of redlining and other discriminatory housing practices, Black Americans and immigrants were forced to live and purchase homes in specific areas and those areas were deemed poor investments and high risk.[7] Therefore those areas were not attractive to commercial business investors which meant fewer job opportunities. They were also cut off from receiving quality health and financial services. These areas were denied quality infrastructure so roads remained filled with potholes and trash went many days without being picked up causing it to leak into the streets.

Many of our families living in urban areas resided in public housing which was also neglected. These units often had inferior plumbing, leaks, and mold that went untreated and electricity that remained out during extreme weather conditions.[8] This, my friends, is a form of torture and is what's referred to as environmental trauma. It was all part of a greater plan to keep us poor, hopeless, and disenfranchised.

This is the environment that some of our parents and grandparents grew up in. This is also the environment in which my mother had to carry a child which I'm sure brought her much anguish.

I'm convinced that some of the members of our baby boomer generation still suffer from this trauma even today. Many have undiagnosed PTSD from growing up in an atmosphere marked by dehumanizing legislation, poverty, and other societal ills. For them, it looks like acting out on fears of scarcity and poverty, or the opposite, growing comfortable with poverty to the point of embracing it. It also looks like having great anxiety regarding the future. For some, escapism became a way to cope with PTSD and unhealed trauma. And all of this showed up in how they parented us. This is how transgenerational trauma continues to manifest itself and what we will discuss further.

My mother and grandmother have always been the hardest-working women I've known. They were entrepreneurs who owned bustling businesses located in the center of downtown Rock Hill, SC. Being located downtown meant they had to watch the Klu

Klux Klan march in the annual parade adorned from head to toe in their full white garb to intimidate Black families. What made this so disturbing was that no one knew who was hiding under those white hoods— it could have been your neighbor, your child's teacher, the mayor, your doctor, etc.

As a child, I can vividly recall my mother and grandmother working from morning to night in their salons. There were many nights they worked until one or two in the morning. This is the work ethic that sometimes comes from being born into a society filled with racial hatred and systematic oppression. They worked twice as hard to keep poverty at bay and steer the remnants of oppression in another direction.

Once as a kid when we spent the summer at my grandmother's house, my cousin and I came up with the bright idea to create a telephone system using old cans and string. We used string to wire the cans together. We turned the cans upside down hoping we could hear each other from across the house. As kids, we saw this as a neat idea. However, when my grandmother arrived home from standing on her tired feet all day she saw a bunch of string hanging from the chandelier and cans all over the kitchen. In a fury, she yelled at us breaking down in tears for making such a mess of the house. She tore the strings down and demanded we go outside to give her peace. This is an example of how my mother and grandmother often appeared to be easily irritated and on edge. They seemed hardened, overworked, and on guard; If anyone attempted to cross them or disrespect them in the slightest, they made sure to let them know about it and handle it in a way that ensured that it never occurred again. There was never a time I saw them let anything go.

Then there were times when they seemed overwhelmed by life and the obstacles that came attached. It appeared that they were dissatisfied and their joy was stolen.

Because life was difficult, they held great regard for the expectations they placed on us– the children and grandchildren. They wanted us to have a better life than their own so they made sure we lived up to their expectations. To correct us and keep us on the right path, they were brash, outspoken, and sometimes emotionally damaging. I often felt as if I had to walk on eggshells around them because the smallest incident would guarantee a tough reprimand whether it was a spanking with a switch, a hit with a shoe, or a severe verbal lashing. What this manifested in me was severe anxiety. As I grew in age, the anxiety grew with me and presented itself during our marriage.

Their behavior is the side effect of a larger issue. Transgenerational trauma—when the social, emotional, and mental experiences of parents affect the development of their children —and even their grandchildren. Symptoms include anxiety, PTSD, mistrust, anger, low self-esteem, and cycles of trauma such as abuse, addictions, and depression.[9]

Transgenerational trauma not only involves the behavior adapted from parenting. It also includes the traits distributed through genetics. Typically, when we see a child we look to see which parent the child looks like and which features the child absorbs that resemble each parent. "She has a smile just like her mother," we often say as we gaze at the child. Rarely do we take notice of the emotional issues the child inherits from its parents because those are the traits that are more difficult to see.

In addition, there are things a child inherits in utero as well from their parents that have a tremendous impact on the child's makeup. The Association of Psychological Science states, "As a fetus grows, it's constantly getting messages from its mother. It's not just hearing her heartbeat and the music she might play to her belly; it also gets chemical signals through the placenta. A new study finds that this includes signals about the mother's mental state."[10]

This past summer, I fancied myself a gardener. I bought the soil, the seeds, and the risers and went for it. I was so excited to start this as I saw it as a new hobby for me. However, I failed to educate myself before the start. I wasn't aware that the conditions and the type of soil I was using would have a direct impact on the development of the produce and greenery I was planting. I planted many of the items in the wrong fertilizer as I had no idea that I needed to test the soil first. Some items I planted too early, others I planted too late in the Spring. Some items I watered too much and others were not watered enough. The result was that some of my vegetation never ripened while the produce had a strange taste to it. Needless to say, I no longer garden. So it is with us. The conditions in which we arrive will have an impact on how we show up and do life. Studies have proven that if a child is carried while the mother is facing stress, pressure, depression, or poverty that will have an impact on the child.

Just as the garden I was growing was impacted by the soil, fertilizer, and environment around it, so were you as you were developing in utero. As you were in your mother's belly, you experienced the mental state of your mother:

- The feelings she had about birthing a child in a land filled with racism and oppression
- The stress of the relationship she may have had with your father at the time
- The uncertainty and concerns she may have had about her pregnancy
- The fears she may have had about you and her future
- The financial distress she may have been experiencing

If any of these were present, please know that they may have played a part in your development in utero. As stated in developmentelscience.com, "pregnant women's high levels of anxiety are correlated with later problems in children, including a difficult temperament, behavioral and emotional problems, anxiety, problems with attention regulation, impulsivity and hyperactivity, immune functioning, and autoimmune disease, cognitive problems, and stress regulation."[11]

Let's delve deeper into this. Our mothers experienced the emotional stress of their mothers in utero which impacted their emotional development. Same for our grandmothers and so on and so on. Therefore, today, I'm quite sure many of us are still experiencing the emotional distress of our ancestors who were brought to this country as slaves centuries ago. Take for example the young women slaves that were forcibly impregnated and brutally raped by the hand of their slave masters on the plantation to breed more slaves. While carrying their child, these women knew that at some point the child they would birth would not be able to experience the love and happiness that they should in this world. They had to carry the burden of knowing that their child would be abused, raped, bought, and sold as property. As a mother myself, I can't imagine the pain and emotional anguish that those fears brought to our ancestors. However, their emotional distress did not die with them. It still lives inside of us today in the form of transgenerational trauma. And transgenerational trauma causes us to create unhealed emotional wounds in the ones we love.

Questions for Reflection

1. List any significant incidents that occurred in your family. How do you believe these situations had an impact on your family? How do you believe this had an impact on you?

2. Describe any cycles or repeated patterns of behavior you have noticed in your family.

Chapter 3

Hypervigilance

After a traumatic experience, the human system of self-preservation seems to go onto permanent alert, as if the danger might return at any moment.
Judith Lewis Herman, *Trauma and Recovery: The Aftermath of Violence - From Domestic Abuse to Political Terror*

Nijiama

When I owned an event planning business, much of what I coordinated was weddings. If you've ever planned weddings for a living you may be able to relate to what I'm about to share. As the business grew, I dealt with many brides who wanted a lot of services for nothing. They often requested discounts and were ready to haggle about prices while still expecting a very high level of service. If you gave them a discount, they would request an even larger discount. After they exceeded their budget, they would drum up erroneous complaints against your services in attempts to retrieve some of their money back after full services had been rendered. This brought a great deal of stress to my life. After experiencing this way too many times, I became hypervigilant. At the least sign of a bridezilla or any inkling of feeling that someone was ready to stiff me on the bill, I would launch into fight mode and was ready to give them a piece of mind.

On one occasion, a bride called to ask why something she requested at her wedding wasn't handled in the way in which she had envisioned. Instead of hearing her out and taking the time to have a calm and professional conversation with her, I became irate. I was loud, talking over her, refusing to listen to anything she had to say. I was so irate during my conversation that the landlord of the studio that I was leasing as my showroom came to see if I was okay. The issue was that I didn't have inner peace because of my previous history of dealing with difficult brides. Therefore my brain was quick to assume that she was coming to attack me. So when she came with concerns I took all of my past hurts in this area out on her. I was, by all accounts, hypervigilant. I was a hot mess!

Hypervigilance occurs when our brain is constantly on high alert as it is searching for perceived threats that it believes will cause us physical or emotional harm. This state of high alert causes hormones to be released more frequently than necessary in our body which activates our sympathetic nervous system. This system prepares our body to stay and fight it out, flee the situation, or freeze (fight, flight, or freeze). Hypervigilance causes us to be on guard all of the time. It causes us to overanalyze and overreact to almost everything. It fills us with a lack of trust and prevents us from giving people the benefit of the doubt.[1]

Hypervigilance is one of the traits of transgenerational trauma that we have inherited. The violence against our ancestors changed our DNA and made our community more susceptible to hypervigilance. It is the reason why we fear being the only Black family in a public restaurant. It is one of the reasons why we may be ready to set it off when we feel we are being profiled. It is also the cause for which we worry when driving along dark roads in rural southern states, or show concern that our children may face biases in their classrooms from non-Black teachers. The pain of our ancestors still dwells inside of us.

Much like Charlotte above, when Shamon and I were first married, I was in a constant state of hypervigilance. It was passed down to me genetically and exasperated by unhealed emotional wounds. I was easily irritated and I took a lot of things personally. When someone offended me or rubbed me the wrong way, I could feel the emotions arise inside of me. The offense ignited the fight response that I saw in my mother and grandmother. When I was offended, I had to put them in their place by speaking loudly, talking over them, and hitting them as far below the belt as I could. The slightest misunderstandings would cause me to react and overreact. I was always ready to set it off using my words as weapons. I would disregard friendships quickly as if they were disposable for the smallest slight and retaliate for the tiniest infractions.

After a long day at work, I arrived home to discover that CVS Pharmacy failed to tell me that they ran out of the prescription medication that I desperately needed. When I discovered this I lashed out at the customer service rep on the phone, hung up on her, and prepared to drive to the store to give them all a piece of my mind. Suddenly, Shamon stopped me in my tracks and asked, "What good is that going to do other than get yourself arrested and ruin your future? For some reason, you are always ready to fight it out as if you have been bullied all of your life." At that moment it was as if a light bulb had gone off and I realized then that I had a problem that I needed to address or else I would find myself in trouble with the law which would destroy my future or in a deadly situation.

As Black Americans, since we set foot on this land we have had to fight. We have fought to be viewed as humans, we have fought for our rights, we have fought for inclusion yet, we must ask ourselves– have we healed from all of this? Although we are the first generation to embrace self-care as a lifestyle and to make therapy visits a part of our overall healthcare plan there are so many other things that we need to address, root out, and destroy that are impacting us still to this day and hypervigilance is just one of them.

Hypervigilance, which is no doubt chronic stress has been known to cause hypertension and cardiovascular issues. This is one of the reasons our community is much more susceptible to these types of illnesses.[2]

Growing up in my family, no one discussed feelings and emotions. No one exemplified healthy conflict resolution skills. As a child, I saw lots of cursing, yelling, gossiping, and other dangerous behavior, particularly during my mother and stepdad's divorce. So this is the behavior I drew on to resolve conflict in my marriage. This is toxic-learned behavior and it is the type of behavior that we adopt when we are owned by hypervigilance.

When life gets tough, particularly marriage, as humans we look for an exit– flight. As I considered my options during the worst parts of our marriage, I realized that I had to also look at the flight response because I exhibited that behavior as well. I have noticed in the past when things grew uncomfortable for me I would flee. When I was bullied as a child at school, I fled to another school. When things didn't pan out at college as planned, I fled and enrolled in another college. When I disagreed with the manager I worked for, I began searching for a new job. A friend said something I didn't like, I fled the relationship by distancing myself. That's the thing about hypervigilance. It makes you believe you are finding peace however it prohibits you from addressing the issues and healing. So I carried the unresolved pain into the next situation.

For many of us, we revert to freeze when our hypervigilance intertwines with our self-esteem. During my twenties, after graduating from college I attended a career fair. As I was about to walk through the door I saw the room filled with professional employers. Immediately I turned around and drove home. I panicked or went into freeze mode and could not move forward.

I also can recall a time when I owned an event planning business and a representative from one of the largest government consulting firms in the Washington, DC area contacted me about utilizing my services for a huge breakfast they were hosting for their employees. Fear ran through my body like a stream and I could not bring myself to return the phone call. "I'm too small of a person to do this type of work and they will recognize it," is what I thought to myself.

The freeze response is crippling and holds us back from achieving our goals. Some may interpret this as laziness but it's the product of a much larger issue– transgenerational trauma and hypervigilance. Procrastination, lack of follow through, and silence can all be forms of the freeze response. It's difficult to achieve when you are suffering on the inside from pain you can't articulate or understand.

Questions for Reflection

1. Select the response you typically choose when you are stressed– fight, flight, or freeze– in each setting below. Please add specific examples:
   - Professional spaces
   - Family settings
   - Friends and acquaintances
   - Community-church and social organizations

Chapter 4

Parenting Wounds

"If your parents' faces never lit up when they looked at you, it's hard to know what it feels like to be loved and cherished. If you come from an incomprehensible world filled with secrecy and fear, it's almost impossible to find the words to express what you have endured. If you grew up unwanted and ignored, it is a major challenge to develop a visceral sense of agency and self-worth."
— **Bessel A. van der Kolk,** ***The Body Keeps the Score: Brain, Mind, and Body in the Healing of Trauma***

Nijiama

Charlotte was born and raised by a no-nonsense single mother, Janice, in Newark, NJ. In addition to Charlotte, Janice had two other children. Outspoken and brazen Janice rarely smiled and took everything seriously. She did not hug yet she doled out strict instructions for the children to follow each day. Lack of compliance with those instructions resulted in stiff consequences such as being cursed out or spanked.

Because Janice worked long hours picking up extra shifts to cover the essentials, Charlotte had to take care of her younger siblings. Every morning, she helped them get dressed for school. When school was out in the summer, it was Charlotte who prepared breakfast, lunch, and sometimes dinner. If Charlotte wanted to visit her friends, her siblings had to accompany her. When her mother went out for the evening, she had to spend the evening tending to the children. When her mother entertained overnight guests, Charlotte had to keep the children quiet and out of the way.

Subconsciously, Charlotte held lots of resentment towards her mother for the childhood she lost–parentification. As an adult, these wounds interrupted their bond. The life advice her mother tried to give her, Charlotte resented. The wound was so raw every disagreement between the two resulted in Charlotte aiming to get her mother to acknowledge the grief she caused. Refusing to admit any wrongdoing, Janice responded with a long list of the things she provided during her childhood; a roof over her head, clothes on her back, food on the table, etc. Many times, these disagreements left months of silence between the two.

Charlotte's feelings towards her mother bled into other areas of her life. Charlotte found it a challenge to deal with authority and manage her emotions. She resented being told what to do by anyone and became irate when she felt choices were taken away from her. Criticism was hard for her to accept. She was easily irritated by the minor annoyances of her female friends and took almost everything personally.

Like Charlotte, many adults are still dealing with the wounds from our childhood including myself. Some circumstances occurred during childhood that shaped our perspective and even impacted our sense of self. Truth is, it's not what happens to us, it's often how we deal with what happens to us that matters the most, and familial pains that occurred during our childhood often remain unprocessed, unhealed, or misinterpreted. It's interesting how the things that occurred to us decades ago have such a profound impact on our present-day lives.

I can vividly recall when my mother and stepfather planned to get married. We all moved into a house together and I was told there would be a wedding in which I would be a flower girl. No one asked what my thoughts were about this or how it made me feel. I simply had to get on board.

Initially, it was awkward and weirdly uncomfortable. I had to make space for a new person who was now embedded in our everyday lives— eating dinner with us, making decisions for us, sharing the refrigerator with us, riding in the car with us, etc. Some of the practices my mother and I had when it was just the two of us had to change and I had to find my way through the transition– alone. This is when I began to internalize my feelings. Soon internalizing became the way I handled most of my hurts. I spent so much time overthinking situations while developing conclusions that may or may not have been true. Eventually, I grew up to become an adult who acted out on internalized feelings.

As a child, though, my behavior became a reflection of how I was feeling inside; It was my way of illustrating the words I was afraid to say to my family. So it looked like, writing on furniture with crayons because I was hungry for attention I wasn't receiving. I'd put on a performance every time visitors came around because I wanted to be noticed to combat feeling as if I didn't matter. I would cry habitually when my favorite cousin's visit ended because I spent so much time alone.

In the past, in our community, when the elders saw a child acting out they may have labeled that child as "bad" or "fast" instead of getting to the root of the issue. Often parenting favored dishing out stiff punishments over having meaningful conversations with children because of fear of the backlash. It may be difficult for a parent to hear their child say that the divorce caused them trauma, that mommy's new boyfriend makes them feel uncomfortable, or that the way daddy behaves when he is drinking is embarrassing. So these things are left unsaid.

When some of our parents were frustrated with our behavior, words were often used to cause harm as if our community had somehow embraced the notion that we must hurt a child's feelings to correct their behavior. Growing up in my family, harsh words were used to correct behavior and those words were painful. I can recall hearing a distant cousin say to his one and only son in the heat of the moment, "You ain't nothing and you ain't going to be nothing, you dummy!" Although those words were not directed at me, I still felt them and I know they had an impact on my cousin.

As a mom, it pains me to admit there was a time when I believed this was good parenting and used it myself– there I go passing down transgenerational trauma. It was during a moment when my daughter spilled red juice onto the light carpet after I told her several times to keep the juice away from the carpet that I found myself in a bout of rage ready to chastise her with my words. At that moment, I looked into my daughter's innocent eyes and realized that I did not want her to experience the pain that I felt as a kid. I understood this was poor behavior on my part. Particularly using language laced with profanity aimed directly at a child, regardless of the reason, damages the child. A parent moves from advocate to adversary very quickly when they attack a child with harmful words– the epitome of emotional abuse.

This type of parenting lasted well into my teenage years. No one ever asked for my opinions on the type of school I wanted to attend or the clothes I wanted to wear. I was told what to do and how to do it. If I didn't comply, there were stiff consequences. It's interesting how our families take the voice and reason away from children and teenagers but expect us to switch it on automatically and make rational decisions when we become young adults. Because of this, as an adult, I spent many years second-guessing my decisions. I often had to see what someone else was doing before I made my own decision. Wise decision-making is a skill that I had to learn to develop on my own as well as learn to trust myself. Self-love begins with trusting ourselves.

These wounds spilled over into my marriage. When I raised my voice at Shamon, it was my eight-year-old inner child screaming to be heard. When I cursed him out, it was my frustrated inner child hoping to be understood.

For a while, I was angry with my family because of the way they raised me. To heal this wound, I had to stop reacting to my family and start with compassion and understanding who they were and why they showed up the way they did.

This process began with realizing that the notion of childhood was very different now than what it was generations ago. For my grandparents who were raised in the 30s and 40s, childhood wasn't something that was honored and revered. It wasn't a time of nurturing, play, and being carefree as it is now. The Fair Labor Standards Act that made child labor illegal was not passed until 1938 so my grandparents spent much of their childhood working to help support the family. Even after child labor laws were passed, many of our elders spent their childhood heavily immersed in household chores– cleaning clothes on washboards, hanging clothes on clotheslines, chopping wood for fires to keep the house warm in the winter, and so forth. And this belief continued to be part of how they raised their children.[1]

If you were a child at any time between the 1950s and 1990s, please understand that you were quite possibly being raised by people who were born during a very difficult time in history for Black Americans—the Civil Rights Era. In 1963, the unemployment rate was 5% for whites but almost 11% for Blacks. In the 1970s, Blacks continued to be more than twice as likely to work in service jobs as white men who held professional roles which was reflected in earnings.[2]

During the Civil Rights era, our country was under the leadership of racists who proudly touted their hateful values. Former President Dwight D. Eisenhower, who was in office from 1953-1961, commented to Chief Justice Earl Warren during a White House Dinner that he could understand why White southerners wanted to make sure "their sweet little girls [are not] required to sit in school alongside some big black buck."[3]

In the South, staunch segregationists such as Senators Harry Byrd, Strom Thurmond, and James Eastland stood firmly against the Civil Rights Movement. They defended white identity by encouraging engagement in massive resistance against laws that desegregated schools such as Brown vs Board of Education.[4]

Therefore, poverty was very much so present, racism was a value, and high-earning employment opportunities were difficult for our elders to obtain. Daily, being pitted against race-based systems that were developed to keep us disenfranchised and oppressed–racial trauma– caused them anger, grief, depression, and hypervigilance. This all impacted how our families parented.

Because times were so difficult, many of us, as children, heard the word "no" more than we would have liked to or should have heard it. A former colleague mentioned that his parents divorced around his eighth birthday. Money was tight and his mother had to work long hours. As a kid, he mentioned that anything he asked for or wanted to do that involved money or his parents' time was met with an automatic no. As he put it, the word no was on speed dial in his home. I certainly can relate to this. For our parents, if no wasn't due to financial hardships, or the lack of time, they believed it was the means of preparing us for the harsh world. Yet hearing no often left us to wonder–am I deserving of anything good? Whew! That's a tough feeling to live with y'all. And it causes us to feel less than worthy. The struggle to find worth within ourselves is a joy-stealing pain that can haunt us for all of the days that we roam the earth– until we heal.

With the burden being so heavy on their shoulders, many parents didn't carve out the time to affirm us. Some of us never heard how handsome we were, how beautiful we were, how smart we were, or how important we were at home. Self-esteem has to be built and when it's not established in our home it leaves us to do things we believe to gain the affirmation we crave. So in our minds, we think:

✓ *If I dress like *insert name of pop culture icon*, people will see me.*
✓ *If I buy an expensive car, people will notice me.*
✓ *Wearing makeup will cause people to tell me I'm pretty.*

✓ *If I buy the big house everyone will see I have accomplished something.*
✓ *Acquiring a certain career will show everyone I have value.*

Focusing on gaining attention prevents us from fulfilling our purpose and doing things that truly make a difference. Regardless of the amount of compliments we gain, it will never be enough to fill us up. The window of time our parents had to build our self-esteem has been missed. Although others can supplement the work we are doing on ourselves, no one outside of us will ever be able to do what our parents were supposed to do.

We also have to realize that if our parents did not get their emotional needs met as children they may show up as emotionally immature. This looks like slamming doors, lashing out when they feel unheard, and doling out the silent treatment. They may also use money and resources as a weapon. Many of us have heard our parents state:

You are going to need me one day.

I did *insert any random act of kindness* for you. Don't forget it!

This is not only emotionally immature behavior but also manipulation. We as healing adults have to understand that when a person doesn't have healthy tools and they are fighting their demons this can be the behavior they rely on. It has nothing to do with us as the child but everything to do with them. That's why we must heal so we do not internalize it, making it our issue.

Questions for Reflections

1. What are some major changes/transitions that occurred during your childhood? How did they impact you?

2. Describe discipline in your home as a child.

3. If you are a parent today, what methods do you use to discipline your child? Is there anything you feel you should change after reading this?

4. List a few of the compliments that you like to receive.
   How did these compliments make you feel? Why do you believe they have such an impact on you?

Momma Trauma

Nijiama

Do you remember the episode of *The Cosby Show* in which Vanessa and her friends journeyed to Baltimore to attend a concert without their parent's permission? In that episode, after the girls are caught, Claire Hanks Huxtable, mother of Vanessa, lunged at a remorseful Vanessa as if she was about to snatch her soul out of her body.[1] Whew! If you watched Netflix's *Roxanne Roxanne* you saw a no-nonsense single mother, played by actress Nia Long, who cursed, fussed, and threatened to not allow her children to enter her home after a certain time.[2] This behavior can be typical of Black moms and many of us have seen it.

Our mothers are the first to demonstrate love to us, protect us, and provide for us. Depending on how they loved us determines how we love and maneuver through our relationships. It also determines how we love ourselves.

During slavery, Black families were severed. In many instances, enslaved fathers were sold and removed from families because it made for submissive female slaves.[3] This also ensured that male slaves understood that their primary responsibility was to labor for the owner. Additionally, with the father being absent it removed a layer of protection for the enslaved families. Therefore, slave owners could do as they pleased to the female slaves without the fear of any type of recourse.

The separation of the Black family during slavery combined with the oppression in the aftermath pierced a sword through our families that would last for decades. It made relating to each other difficult as Black men perceived their absence from the family to cause minimal damage. And when poverty arose, which it did, they believed the best thing to do for the family was to leave as it made for one less mouth to feed. Therefore, many Black mothers became the head of the family thus creating the alpha mom. Being the sole provider forced Black women to become tough and removed the softness that comes with femininity. Some women passed this down to their daughters.

My dear sisters, please don't kill me for saying this but we have to be honest with ourselves and own our part in the angry black woman stereotype just as we want our white female counterparts to own the karen stereotype. The angry black woman trope plagues us but there is a hint of truth to it. Often when a Black woman becomes upset or feels disrespected, we can expect anything from a hostile attitude to a full rage to follow shortly after. Don't believe me? Search any social media platform and there will be many images and videos of Black women displaying ill-tempered behavior, destroying property in airports, fighting on cruise ships during what should be vacation time, cursing out restaurant servers, and so forth.

How many times have we heard a Black woman say any of the following:
He/she has the right one today!
I'm not to be played with!
You're gonna learn today!

I bet we have all heard a fellow Black woman explain how they popped off/clapped back/went ham on someone. I've even said these things myself. This is because our unresolved trauma passed down from slave ancestry causes us to become hypervigilant, similar to Charlotte. The hypervigilance ignites the fight response because there have been times historically when we have had no other choice than to do so. Anger is in our DNA and it's the response we result to when we are frustrated. Not only have we resulted to this behavior but our community has fully embraced it.

For Black mothers, some of this shows up in parenting. Many Black mommas are strong, tough, and very direct. For the moms that were abrasive, as kids, we would say, "his/her mom doesn't play!"

There is a link between hypervigilance and anxiety.[4] The fears they had about life and unresolved trauma caused many moms to become overprotective. Their parenting was sometimes led by fear and that, often, felt smothering. They wanted the best for us, but their toughness and harsh demeanor sometimes made childhood a challenge.

If we have been parented by this type of mother we may find that we welcome friends who embrace toxic behavior such as lashing out, telling people off, and even fighting. This is because we have dealt with it for so long, we have become used to it. We have the bandwidth for it whereas others who did not grow up that way may have a hard time accepting this type of behavior because it's so foreign to them.

Trauma unhealed can cause us to become cynical and easily triggered. Our mothers have dealt with their share of trauma and emotional hurts. Whether it was being a victim of overt racism, dealing with the death of a loved one, experiencing a divorce or dissolution of a relationship, or managing poverty, our mothers did not have the means or time to properly process their pain. They had children to provide for and responsibilities to handle so they tucked away their emotions and continued with their routine. Those hurts did not go away. Instead, they resurfaced when they were triggered and as children, many times we pulled the trigger.

My mother was and still is a very strict alpha mom, lord have mercy. As a child, my mom was very particular about her children and made sure that we always appeared neat, clean, well-mannered, and well-dressed. Our hair always had to be freshly styled and our shoes always had to be clean. She never wanted us to give the appearance of poverty. Black mothers, much like my own, knew that White America deemed our race as a whole undesirable thus they never wanted us to appear to be the most undesirable of the undesirables. Out of this notion, assimilation was birthed, and its elements such as code-switching to prove that we were safe for them—and not like the others.

As a teenager and adult, this had quite an impact on me. I spent lots of time worrying about my appearance and attire, never believing that I was enough without the "glam". I would spend my last dime on the trendiest of clothes, hair relaxers, weaves, wigs, styles, and the list goes on and on. If there was a party, you can best believe I was going to the mall before the event to purchase a new outfit to wear. Now don't get me wrong there is absolutely nothing wrong with caring about your appearance and having a desire to look nice, however, do you feel just as good without the glitz and glam? I can recall being at parties and events looking at how all of the other girls were dressed and feeling as if I didn't measure up in some way. I would question myself:

Is my weave long enough?
Are my pants tight enough?
Is my butt big enough?
Is my outfit cute enough?

Questions for Reflection

1. What was your mother's attitude towards your
    appearance as a child? How did this shape
    your attitude towards these things as an adult?

2. Describe your feelings towards your mother
    when you were a child.

3. Describe your feelings towards your mother
    today.

Poppa Was a Rolling Stone

Nijiama

When I think of Black fathers my mind automatically thinks of Heathcliff Huxtable. Regardless of Bill Cosby's actions, the character Heath Cliff Huxtable showed us what involved parenting looks like. And I'm grateful that I know many men who parent in a very similar manner today.

Let's be real here, we all know that many dads haven't always embraced the Heathcliff Huxtable ideal. Some chose to be emotionally unavailable. Perhaps they prided themselves on being the provider and protector like Jared's dad but didn't find value in nurturing their children's emotions. Others chose to be tough or embrace the idea of being a "rolling stone", or just not present at all. There are a myriad of reasons and excuses. Understand that these situations aren't unique to Black men but all men.

According to the Children's Research and Family Institute at the University of Texas Austin, "Involved fatherhood is linked to better outcomes on nearly every measure of child well-being, from cognitive development and educational achievement to self-esteem and pro-social behavior. Children who grow up with involved fathers are 39% more likely to earn mostly A's in school, 45% less likely to repeat a grade, 60% less likely to be suspended or expelled from school, twice as likely to go to college and find stable employment after high school, 75% less likely to have a teen birth, and 80% less likely to spend time in jail ."[1]

One of the first steps in building a home is setting up the foundation. This is one of the most important aspects of homebuilding because the structural integrity of the home rests on a firm foundation. If the foundation is firm, the home can last forever. So it is with having a present and emotionally available father. They serve as the foundation for our lives. They fill young girls with confidence and help young men gain identity and a sense of self-worth.

Having a healthy relationship with dad is especially important for women. Girls tend to view their dad as their superhero, placing him on a pedestal. If dad fails to build healthy interactions with his daughter it can cause low self-esteem. It can be empowering for a woman to have the superhero of her life, give him her name, spend time with her, show up for her, and protect her.

Unavailable fathers missed the opportunity to teach their sons how to manage stress and pressure. Psychological studies show time and time again that boys who grow up without their fathers are likely to be quicker to anger and struggle with low self-esteem.[2] For these young men raised without a father, the wound is still raw and has left its imprint on their soul causing them to question–am I good enough? For them, these wounds make every offense, even the minor ones, a priority causing them to react and overreact. These reactions include lashing out quickly when offended, holding grudges as a weapon, and tit-for-tat behavior.

The foundation of a home also serves as protection as well. It keeps moisture out and insulates from the cold. Fathers also serve as protection. They protect not only physically but emotionally. When the father is not in the home, the children feel less than safe and may strive to take on the role of protector.

The Children's Bureau of Southern California states fatherless children are five times more likely to have experienced physical abuse and emotional maltreatment, with a one hundred times higher risk of fatal abuse.[2] Fathers, our soul-protecting superheroes are necessary. However, they must be healed and emotionally available when they show up or else their presence can cause more harm than good.

Aside from my stepfather, some of the men surrounding me as a kid were womanizers. These men had affairs and caused lots of heartache to the women they made vows to honor and respect. Some also chose not to be present fathers to their children. What this type of parenting produced was emotionally ill sons and daughters, like Lauren, who hungered for emotional connection from men. Please know that the relationship that was absent from our lives as children we tend to crave in our adulthood. Each child goes through development stages and affirmation is needed from both parents in these stages. Involvement from both parents has a tremendous impact on brain development and how a person perceives themselves. Rejection and feeling less than worthy causes lots of inner chaos that can present in adults as emotionally needy, easily angered, and constantly seeking affirmation.

As a young woman, because I saw men behaving poorly towards women, I accepted this same type of behavior from men during my early dating experiences. I didn't like it and of course, I argued and complained about it but I remained in these types of relationships because that's what was familiar to me. There were many times during my early dating experiences that I believed I had standards yet I made choices to settle for less.

When we grow up without healthy men in our lives, we don't understand the values we should identify in a partner. So we allow society, media, and our peers to dictate the type of partners we should date. I dated the guy with three kids by three different baby mommas because his swag was so powerful to me that I was willing to turn a blind eye to the red flags. I dated the drug dealer who had limited education and lacked professional ambition because he was good-looking and drove a nice car. I remained attracted to the cute guy who wasn't fully invested in me because his lack of emotional availability wasn't a turn-off to me—it was familiar.

Hypervigilance plays a role in this as well. Toxic relationships cause a release of dopamine and adrenaline while activating the body's stress response system. These types of relationships seem thrilling. The chemical release makes these relationships addictive as we crave the high from lust and drama. Soon, peaceful relationships appear boring. Messy, toxic love becomes a habit-forming pattern.[3]

****

As we are working to heal our parenting wounds, for those of us with families of our own, we have to be mindful of how we parent. Often we parent with a focus on giving our children all of the things we didn't get as children and trying so hard to overly protect them from harm. I began to notice I was trauma parenting which means I was parenting from a place of fear and my traumas instead of parenting from love, hope, and grace. So for me that looked like fearing allowing my children to play outside without me constantly watching them and being afraid to allow them to visit their friend's homes. It was also being too nervous to allow them to attend the school field trip if I couldn't attend, and not allowing them the freedom to explore, be independent, and make their own mistakes. It was surrounded by a constant feeling that trouble was around the corner. This is also anxiety that causes us to smother love and trauma parent our children– completely unhealthy. This was a product of my inner child wounds and the inherited hypervigilance impacting my parenting– generational trauma.

Questions for Reflection

1. Have your parents healed from their wounds?

2. Describe a situation in which you accepted poor treatment from a romantic partner. Why do you believe you accepted it?

3. Describe a situation in which you treated a romantic partner or interest poorly.
   o Why do you believe you treated them this way?
   o How do you think this impacted them?
   o How do you think you could have handled it differently?

Action Items

List five core values you believe are important in a romantic partner.

The Wounds of Masculinity

Shamon

As a kid in my community, the definition of manhood and masculinity was very stereotypical – Tough, rough, athletic, rap music-loving, wearing baggy clothes and the latest Nikes and Jordans, and spending lots of time chasing women. That is what a man's man was considered to be where I came from.

As kids that definition played a big role in who we chose as friends. Most of us played basketball at the courts all day or tossed the football around in the street. We took notice of the boys who chose not to do those things as they weren't considered masculine. Sadly, many were called derogatory names such as nerd, sissy, or punk.

This causes men to question themselves– If I do not fit my community's definition of manhood does that mean something is wrong with me? Or if I am more sensitive and creative and prefer not to throw a football or chase women all day does that make me less masculine than others?

I completely agree with the late great bell hooks when she states that we need to redefine what it means to be a man in our community and that means widening the definition. Masculinity should not be defined by how far one can throw a ball or how many women one dates.[1]

This narrow definition of manhood has been embraced in our community and to reinforce the idea that men should be tough, some Black fathers were not warm to their sons. There was not a lot of hugging, kissing, and vulnerable conversation. This is how the breeding of generations of emotionally unavailable men continues.

For men, the yearning to be validated by an emotionally and physically involved father never leaves. As in the example of Jared, the source of his bragging was not about the things he accomplished, or what he spent his time doing but about the affirmation and approval he could gain by mentioning those things. People do not brag just for the sake of bragging. Often, they brag with the hopes of receiving the kudos they needed as a child. They may also brag to shape the perspective of others which is something they felt they could not do in the past.

Many of us have known someone with a personality very similar to Jared's. In his relationship with his father, some things happened or didn't happen that made him feel as though his father didn't approve or value him. It could have been his father's lack of emotional availability, criticism from his father, or a disagreement they had. Regardless of the cause, he never felt he had a father who believed he was enough just as he is. So, this became the thing that motivated him to excel.

As an adult, Jared spends his time attempting to gain approval from people whose validation really shouldn't matter. The pain becomes evident when he is deeply hurt by those who do not rise to give him the approval that he seeks or those who choose not to buy into his lectures or the belief that he is anything short of what he wants you to believe. His unhealed emotions translate this into rejection. And once he feels rejected, he will retaliate. For him, his retaliation usually consists of rejecting the person who he feels rejected him. You've heard the statement hurting people hurt people. Well, rejected people reject people. Now some may view his behavior as petty. But there is a reason behind the pettiness and usually, it stems from a tremendous disappointment from a caregiver that went unhealed.

Often a person similar to Jared will build relationships with those whom he deems safe—those who need him, who will always agree with him, and who he subconsciously believes to be inferior to him in some type of way. He knows he will always shine amongst them thus giving him the ego boost and validation he desires.

If we face trauma in our early development years, it may be difficult to strike the right balance in relationships. We may sometimes get too close or not allow people to get close enough. That was me. I built a wall surrounding me that was very high. I kept quite a bit of myself hidden from the world. It was my way of protecting myself. It was also my way of maintaining masculinity as I was conditioned to do.

As a father myself, I need to be self-aware of my own emotions so that I can understand and guide the emotions of my children. I've had to learn to be in tune with their emotions and to allow them space to share their hearts. This is intimacy– what I needed in my early years.

Questions for Reflection

1. What are some of the positive values your father possessed?

2. What did you need from your father as a child that you did not get? How did it impact you?

3. What do you believe you need as an adult from your father?

Chapter 5

Childhood Abandonment and Neglect

"We have learned that trauma is not just an event that took place sometime in the past; it is also the imprint left by that experience on mind, brain, and body. This imprint has ongoing consequences for how the human organism manages to survive in the present. Trauma results in a fundamental reorganization of the way the mind and brain manage perceptions. It changes not only how we think and what we think about, but also our very capacity to think."
— **Bessel A. van der Kolk,** *The Body Keeps the Score: Brain, Mind, and Body in the Healing of Trauma*

Nijiama

Tesa was a girl I knew in my younger years in South Carolina. Our families were friends; my mother knew her mother, my grandmother knew her grandmother, and so on. In high school, she was always very well dressed to the nines and her hair was always freshly styled. She was friendly and popular. By the time she reached the 11th grade, she had a boyfriend who she was seriously invested in. They were the kind of couple that was inseparable; whether it was a sporting event, the cafeteria at school during lunchtime, or at the local grocery store the two of them were always together.

Because our town was small, I would see her rather often. Suddenly, I began to notice I didn't see her as much. I just assumed she was sick. When I did see her, however, I noticed her attire changed to torn and dirty clothing that didn't display her usual neat appearance that I admired. To many, it appeared as if she slowly stopped caring about her appearance. Without fail, I began to hear rumors that the worst had occurred to her– her boyfriend introduced her to crack cocaine and she was now a full-blown addict.

During the late 1970s, the Black community was still dealing with oppression, poverty, and racism. It was at a time in which many of our young men who served in the Vietnam War, returned home with full-blown PTSD to discover they were despised for going to war and found very few job opportunities available for them. It was around this time that many young

Americans were experimenting with recreational drug usage (psychedelics, marijuana, cocaine). Drugs were readily available at parties, dance clubs, recording studios, movie sets, business meetings, and even in some suburban homes. America was dealing with a drug culture that would fill our cities and towns with violence and evil.

As the 80s arose, people continued to party looking for their usual high that helped them to escape the pain of reality. Many were unaware that a modified cheapened version of a major drug was birthed out of the drug culture. This drug struck Black America like a hurricane—crack cocaine.

Times were difficult. I get it. Poverty was present and disappointments appeared inevitable. Recreational drug usage became a way to escape and ease the pain of day-to-day life. What made crack cocaine unique, however, was that it was not only highly addictive but was also cheap enough for people living in urban areas to afford. Because of this, crack became a popular drug amongst inner-city dwellers and with time and gumption, it eventually spread across the country.

In the 1990s, The US Department of Justice stated, "Crack cocaine abuse is the most serious drug problem in Illinois, particularly in Chicago and other urban areas. In 1995, Cook County alone was estimated to have more than 266,000 hardcore cocaine abusers."[1]

According to New York State statistics, there were 182,000 habitual cocaine users in 1986 in New York City. In 1988 that number more than tripled to an estimated total of 600,000 according to city officials.[2]

Hear me out: aside from slavery and its legacy, the most destructive force that happened to our community was the crack cocaine epidemic. I don't believe that people really understand how much we lost to crack cocaine.

As a kid in the '90s, I watched crack spread through my small town like wildfire. It was jarring to see people who I once admired, quite like Tesa, who appeared to have the world at their fingertips disintegrate. The disintegration would begin gradually as the pursuit of the high would make it difficult for them to maintain employment. Eventually, they would disengage from the community. The shame of their behavior, appearance, and disappointment to their loved ones caused them to hide.

As this behavior became common, eventually as a kid, I began to know a crack addict or as we referred to them "crackheads" when I'd see one. In addition to the unkempt appearance, it was the frequent requests for five or ten dollars here and there that were a dead giveaway. If they weren't requesting to "borrow" a few dollars they were asking for a ride because their car was either repossessed or given to a drug dealer in exchange for a high.

In the Black community, crack addicts were the brunt of many jokes. We looked at these individuals as a source of humor as well as a form of low-cost labor. If you needed any type of labor performed one could easily hire an addict to perform it at a very low cost. That's just how it was. Yet we never considered that these individuals who were now the brunt of our jokes or the means of our low-cost labor were someone's mother, father, sister, brother, daughter, or son. As a community, we deemed them insignificant and less than human because of their addiction. So it made it easy to disregard their feelings and make fun of them.

I've watched many people lose their lives to crack cocaine—cousins, classmates, family friends, and more. As a society, we treated these people as if they died. We completely gave up on them. To be honest, some preferred it that way.

Many of these addicts had children before or birthed children during their addiction. The question that we rarely ask is what are the wounds carried by the children of addicts? What are the wounds carried by those who were once addicted?

Several years ago, the organization I was working for was awarded a grant funded by the Washington DC Government. This grant was designed to provide vocational training, along with career, financial, and personal counseling to DC residents who met certain criteria. Most of the individuals that we served under this grant were underemployed Black men and women between the ages of 18-30. I discovered that many of these individuals were the remnants of the crack cocaine epidemic. They were once the neglected children who were either placed in the foster care system, raised by a relative because their parents could no longer look after them, or took to living on their own on the streets. Because for their parents, nothing was more important than the high or the fix. And by its addictive allure, crack cocaine caused them to spend their days and nights chasing it. That's the thing about crack– it's unforgiving and doesn't care about who it leaves behind. Crack cocaine spared no one who gave in to it. If given the chance it would wrap its arms around your mother, father, uncle, grandmother, sister, or next-door neighbor and have its way with them until their lives were completely wrecked.

Because of my work on this particular program, I have seen with my own eyes the destruction that crack cocaine has brought to our communities. I heard many stories of the harshness of being a child of an addicted parent; children who were forced to wear dirty clothes and sweaters during the summer months because their mother failed to do the laundry. Children who were forced to survive on a diet of potato chips and soda pop given to them out of mercy from the local corner store owner because their parents spent the grocery money on drugs. Children who didn't receive proper healthcare because their parents didn't have insurance. Children who didn't learn how to care for their bodies and handle themselves properly outside of the home because there was no one around to educate them. I heard the story of a ten-year-old who was locked outside of the house until the early morning hours while watching her parents smoke crack through a pipe with friends. I listened to the pain of loved ones who watched their family members disappear for days on end without a word.

These individuals are some of the most resilient people I have ever met but what remained was the hypervigilance from having to fend for themselves at such a tender age. Dealing with emotions that never healed such as the pain of having parents that were now the brunt of jokes within the community.

Dealing with a childhood that was stolen from them. This put them in survival mode and self-sabotaging behavior became a way of life. For this reason, there were many days that we were cursed out, and threatened, and some of us were violently attacked.

The worst fear of any child is being abandoned by their parent. Hence the reason babies cling to their parents and cry in their absence. When abandonment and neglect wounds occur, they rewire our brains and cause us to struggle with how we connect or attach ourselves to others. It causes us to enter relationships filled with lots of insecurities because we fear that the people we love will abandon us similar to our parents. We lack trust and may be prone to manipulate out of fear. Consequently, we may be a bit clingy and controlling in our relationships or have a hard time honoring boundaries.

When abandonment and neglect wounds are present, we may attempt to consume all of our romantic partners' time and require our friends to be fully devoted to us only. That can feel smothering to them. We become driven by a constant fear of being abandoned because our parents made us feel so easily disposable.

Abandonment wounds make us easily disappointed. They also take away our ability to recover from disappointment. For the sufferer, every disappointment and minor annoyances from loved ones triggers the unhealed wounds inside of us causing us to lash out.

Sabrina, for example, suffers from abandonment wounds. For many years, she viewed her mother's inability to care for her as abandonment while she additionally struggled with feeling neglected by her family. This caused her to perceive herself to be of lower value and rejection became difficult for her to handle. As an adult, she acted on these feelings. When her boss failed to return her phone call, she grew angry. When friends didn't invite her to lunch, she was hurt. When someone forgot her birthday, she canceled them–because these events felt similar to the multitude of painful disappointments experienced at such a tender age by the adults who failed to be there for her in the way she needed.

Let me tell you that when our caregivers abandon us at a very young age it cuts deep. It not only damages our emotions but it taints our spirit as well. Wounds of this type cause us to lose our innocence as we become cynical so early in life. Empathy becomes very difficult to tap into because we've spent the first part of our lives surviving instead of being carefree and enjoying life as a child. Survival mode places us in a state of hypervigilance putting us constantly in the fight response while making us chronically defensive. The unhealed pain deep inside of us turns to anger. The anger feels like a ball of fire inside of us that screams, "I went through hell as a child, and I shouldn't have!"

So picture this: piles of anger bubbling up inside of the soul impacting emotions. For the anger to release itself often it will attach itself to nasty, evil, and explosive blame. Like a bomb being fired from a cannon, blame will target a victim to assign fault during even the smallest of incidents. Working in conjunction with anger, blame will criticize, condemn, and point out perceived wrongs in the harshest of manners. Blame is the preferred tool for those with abandonment and childhood neglect trauma because it brings a perceived temporary sense of relief. It may feel good to release the pent-up frustrations from a childhood that was lost. However, in its path, it leaves behind destroyed relationships. Because blame is blind, it often targets the people who love us the most and those whom God sent to help us.

As heroin abuse was typically used by men, crack cocaine became an addiction for women.[3] That means that there were numerous children left with a mother wound. Additionally, for those who were raised on the streets and in the foster care system, these children were left to form their own identity without values, principles, or boundaries to live and abide by. This is how we develop generations of young adults who have no regard for their bodies, love, relationships, or themselves. What's worse is that some of the individuals have now become social media and reality TV influencers who are able to dictate the behavior of our youth simply because they have a platform. This is how we continue to pass down the legacy of trauma and pain.

Even on the harshest of days during my work in DC, which happened to be when I was cursed out the most, threatened at best, and when keys were thrown at me barely missing my eyeball by a hair, I would look inside of the person and see the pain. I saw that their actions were the screams of a hurting inner child who did not receive the love and support they needed.

****

My grandparents were the first to build their home on land they purchased in the center of my town in Rock Hill, SC. Soon other middle-class Black families built homes in that area. It was a place where my mother and her siblings played freely in the 1960s with neighborhood children who were like them. It was also a place where people loved and looked out for each other. There were many Black-owned businesses in that area such as the corner store who became familiar with the families within the community. When someone couldn't afford groceries, they still supplied them, accepting pay later. This was community.

In the early 1970s, the city built apartments in that area that were initially considered luxury during that time. To ensure the units were rented quickly, the landlords began to accept government subsidies such as section 8. Very soon, in the 1980s this area became inhabited by crack cocaine. Addicts rambled the streets day and night looking for items to pilfer while local street dealers fought over the turf. This led to lots of gun violence that cost us many lives and destroyed the local businesses that served the area.

What occurred to my grandmother's neighborhood is very similar to what occurred to other once vibrant areas in the '80s and '90s such as Harlem, New York City, Southeast and Northeast Washington, DC, Oakland CA, and Chicago, IL. During the 2000s, investment companies saw an opportunity in our pain as they bought and sold our neighborhoods turning them into places that are unaffordable for the majority. These neighborhoods priced out everything that resembles Black culture such as the local corner stores and soul food eateries as they made way for big box trendy supermarkets and chain coffee shops. Therefore, we must realize that to some degree, we all are the remnants of the crack cocaine epidemic. It robbed us of our communities and destroyed our families. We may not all have parents who were addicted or brothers who were incarcerated due to drug abuse or solicitation but many of us have relatives, friends, and neighbors who were affected in some way thus having an indirect impact on our lives.

Thankfully, many men and women are now on the road to recovery from addiction. Many cities are pouring resources into supporting those who were taken to hell and back due to this drug. However, what remains is the hurt and broken relationships. Many adult children of addiction are frustrated because their loved one refuses to admit the pain they caused. And many in recovery are frustrated that the pain is still raw and remembered.

If you are in recovery, even if it has only been for one day, I'm sure you have climbed through the chambers of hell to get to where you are today. The past is just that but you can now reclaim your present and future. You are now an overcomer and more importantly, you are free. Every clean day should be a day of celebration for you.

Questions for Reflection

1. Describe instances in your childhood in which you felt alone.

2. Which of your needs went unmet during your childhood?

3. Describe a few ways you've been the target of blame.

4. Describe situations in which you have used blame to hurt others.

5. List several ways you have demonstrated resilience over your lifetime.

6. How can you be kinder to yourself?

7. How can you be kinder to your loved one who may have abandoned themselves?

Raised by Mental Illness

Shamon

When my son was five (5) and my daughter was eight (8), I chose to give my son $3 for maintaining good behavior throughout the week. On this rewarding day, my daughter wasn't given the same deal but had wisdom mixed with cunning. My daughter finessed him out of a $1 through some promise to give him some of her things. Initially, he agreed, but then later, I heard my daughter laughing and my son crying. When I came to check on them, what I found was that my son had ripped one of the dollars he was given and another I saw was balled up and thrown into a corner out of anger. The crazy part about this is everything he worked so hard to gain was lost in an instant and his good works were taken and given to his sister. I had to ask myself the question I didn't want to know the answer to, where did he get this behavior from?

I grew up in a very different environment than Nij. While she was raised in the rural south, I was raised in a busy city during the height of the crack cocaine epidemic. The city was filled with concrete sidewalks, makeshift basketball courts, sirens, and an abundance of people in a place called 'Chocolate City' aka Washington, DC.

My mother suffered from mental health disorders, which I'm sure she inherited genetically that I can attribute to many insecurities that seem to pile on moment by moment and year by year. The birth of my sister and I as well as the divorce between her and my father all seemed to mount as pressure for her causing her mental health to fail. These moments were negative triggers that weren't sufficiently addressed since mental health services weren't accessible to people within my community at that time.

When my mother was triggered it would send her into psychosis causing her to fight forces that were not present or unreal, the same as Karen. Her behavior became unpredictable and scary at times.

The thing I learned about severe mental health disorders is that your life becomes disrupted by a domino effect in which one event triggers another event which triggers another until you are left with nothing but the dream of what once was. When the brain is sick, it can appear as if the person is on a quest to destroy every realm of their life including their loved ones. I believe, in these instances, the soul is trying to recover from overwhelming experiences and it often selects behaviors that may appear comforting to them but are harmful.

Just as it is noticeable when a person's other vital organs such as the heart, liver, and lungs are sick, as a kid I could tell when my mother's brain was sick. Her behavior would often become erratic and unpredictable. For example, she would regularly change to a new job. So there were many moments when she gave me a new phone number on a handwritten note as she put the shoestring latchkey around my neck before sending me off for school.

She also became a hoarder of the most random items that we didn't need.

The thing about being raised by a mentally ill parent, you never really know who the real person is. I'd often ask myself, is this behavior who she is? Quite like Karen Brown's family previously mentioned, none of our loved ones knew exactly what to do to help my mother. The only time I heard of someone seeking any form of mental health services was through force by a court order. Legally, people who were deemed insane from my community were put into restraints and forced to undergo treatment at state-run hospitals such as St. Elizabeths. There they were pumped full of one-size-fits-all medication that made them numb and removed their ability to feel. They were also grossly mistreated as racism ran rampant in state hospitals.

With my mother's mental health now being challenged, I was forced to become independent and figure a lot of things out on my own. I was walking to school and riding public transit systems at a very young age so in the neighborhood that I grew up in I had to be tough. I couldn't allow anyone to believe I was weak. Because we lived in such an environment my parents wanted to ensure I was prepared. "Boys aren't supposed to cry," and "Men aren't supposed to be sad about certain losses." This instruction as well as my family issues, left my pain and frustrations to remain welled up inside of me, and to be honest, still to this day vulnerability can sometimes be an issue for me.

These emotions turned to anger (because what doesn't get released often transforms into anger) and it became the dominating force that drove me. Someone would say something about how I dressed, I'd feel a rage well up inside and go into fight mode. I'd be disappointed by the promise of a loved one or friend and there was that anger pulled from the proverbial sheath to start yet another battle or war against the offender who stepped into my mental or physical domain without proper authority. In the end were casualties—friendships ruined, job opportunities gone, relationships stifled, or broken, and in the end its most conspicuous, yet blinding side effect was loneliness.

Looking back at the first few years of our marriage, I realize that anger was the prevailing emotion for me. It had been my way of handling things of the past. So when times were uncomfortable in our marriage I allowed anger to rule which caused me to raise my voice in a very heated situation, to even shove the woman that I had vowed to God to honor and protect.

I held onto anger for quite a while. The thing about anger is that for me, it was so comforting and at the same time empowering. One of the greatest NBA athletes who won multiple championships, along with a host of other accolades used that volatile, explosive emotion to fuel his approach. When given a chance to describe how he became the best at his craft, he said about anger, "I embraced it, and I f****ing loved it." There was no doubt, I could identify with that. That fire seemed to be the awakening of a great power and near invincibility. But, in reflecting, I saw how in those moments it compelled me to action, but the result was loss.

With the anger came the pursuit of peace. When I have a difficult day or a tough dialogue with Nij I immediately need peace afterward. At the beginning of our marriage, peace for me looked like playing video games—this became an outlet, a place where I could take a step away to process my thoughts about situations and develop solutions. Nij didn't understand this. She thought I was running away from her but it was just my way of stepping away to process things. But at that time being so young, I didn't have the language to explain to her that I wasn't running away from her.

Today, I find my peace at the barbershop and my man cave. Those are my spots! In these spaces, I don't feel forced to respond immediately to emails or answer questions. I get to select how I choose to spend the time whether it's watching TV, talking with my barber, working out, or just sitting with my thoughts. I'm rather sure most men hold on to their peaceful outlets whether it's the basketball court or spending copious amounts of time in the basement watching TV and that in itself I suppose is a form of fleeing.

The fight, flight, or freeze response we choose today as adults is based on what is accessible to us in our childhood. For Nij, fighting and fleeing was her way to escape pain. For me, being the son of a mentally ill mother, it's a combination of all three.

Questions for Reflection

1. Think of the last few instances in which you were angry. How did you handle them? What were the results?

2. How has mental illness impacted you and your family?

Chapter 6

You're Smelling Yourself: Dating, Sex, and Intimacy

Solo parents are more than likely to be female and Black.
Pew Research Center

Nijiama

If I had a nickel for every time I heard my grandmother tell us when we were teens, "Don't go out there and get no baby" I'd be rich! In the Black Community, preventing a teen from having sex is like the San Francisco 49ers playing defense in the Super Bowl. Our caregivers were aggressive in trying to keep our hormones at bay. So they used fear and shaming tactics for prevention instead of fully explaining all of the benefits to abstinence. Desperately wanting their children to have a better life than their own, they would do anything they could to prevent teens from having sex too soon. Today, I understand their motives.

When I look back on the time I spent growing up in South Carolina, I realize that most of my friends were the products of single-parent homes, quite like the Brown family mentioned previously. Two-parent homes were rare. As a kid, I saw the struggles that single parenting produced. I now understand why the elders wanted to prevent us from having children too soon with the wrong partner. This was, for many parents, their biggest fear and worst shame. Poverty is often attached to single parenting. The financial and emotional stress combined can be so overwhelming for a single parent that it removes the pleasure of parenting. For a single parent, the strain on their time and finances can feel like oppression.

While working in DC, many of the women we served were single mothers. We saw firsthand the stress that comes with that. Childcare can be so expensive that many have to rely on unlicensed providers to care for their children. Others would wait around in the shadows for our working luncheons to end to gather the scraps to take home for dinner. The stress from unmet desires and unpaid bills would be so overwhelming that it caused anger.

This is what our elders wanted to prevent from occurring in our lives. However, this wasn't always communicated by the elders in the healthiest of ways.

How many of us recall having healthy conversations with our parents about sex and dating as teens? I certainly don't. The conversations about sex that were had in my family were limited to, "Don't have sex", "Boys just want sex", "Don't bring no babies to my house", "don't get that girl pregnant" or "insert name had sex too young and now they are stuck raising a baby." Does this sound familiar to you? Their preventive methods did not work too well because, in a survey that we conducted of a random sample of Black Americans, 64% said they began having sex under the age of eighteen years. I believe that the way the elders handled topics about sex perhaps made us more curious.

When a person enters the preteen to adolescent stage, there is a surge of hormones that causes a teen to desire relationships with the opposite sex as well as become more independent from family. During this time, my grandmother would tell us, "You are smelling yourself," as if the efflux in hormones that we did not create was somehow our fault. Statements such as this made us feel that what we were experiencing was a bad thing. As a teen, it feels awkward to have those feelings and being shunned for it can feel isolating. Our community and society as a whole have normalized scorning teens for "smelling themselves." Instead, we should accept that this is perfectly normal behavior.

Regardless of whether or not I was allowed to have a boyfriend during my teen years, I still had one at that time. I did not share this part of me with my family because I knew they would not approve. This is where the distance between myself and my family began.

I can remember the very first guy I believed I seriously loved during high school. When he and I broke up I was devastated, but I could not tell my family. They would simply say what they always said, which was, "You don't need to worry about boys, focus on those books!" I heard this quite often and it made me feel small and as if my emotions did not matter. It did not stop how I felt, instead, it put a wall between us and impacted how I communicated with them. So, I shut them out and never shared that part of my life with them. My friends, however, were the ones I relied on for support during this time. A bunch of hormonal teens providing life counseling to other hormonal teens is a recipe for disaster.

Because I did not feel comfortable having conversations about love, sex, and intimacy within my family, it left me and many other young people around my age to figure it out on our own. And at that time, many of us believed that dating meant having sex. We were just unaware of any other ways to date and we knew it allowed us to spend time with the boys we were attracted to. As women, we crave closeness because we are relational beings. We saw sex as a means to obtain that so as teenage boys do they asked the girls for sex and it was obliged.

As teens, we didn't know what we were doing though, so we looked to television shows, movies, and other forms of media including porn to figure it out. We also relied on inappropriate touching and various forms of experimenting to understand sex and intimacy. And each of these led us to develop toxic learned behavior that many of us still rely on, even to this day.

A person who may have experimented with porn early on, may continue to view sex through the lens of porn as an adult. Pornography rarely depicts healthy intimacy. The goal of porn is to tap into our darkest desires. Pornography that depicts men with young girls, young boys with older women, aggressive sex, orgies, etc taints our view of romantic sex and intimacy, particularly if we begin viewing it at a young age. Therefore, for example, if a husband tries to bring what he learned from porn to marriage, the wife may not enjoy it. She may crave more intimacy and that can cause a rift in the marriage. Makes sense?

Not to mention the fact that pornography can be addictive. Porn addiction is when there is an insatiable urge to view porn—when one just can't get enough of it. When you need to view porn to gain gratification or before you are intimate with your significant other, there may be an unhealthy addiction. For some reason, these conversations are not being had enough within our community. All of this has a tremendous impact on us and how we show up in committed relationships.

Men and women are conditioned quite differently when it comes to love and romance. For many women, because we have been conditioned to believe that our happily ever after begins with romance, typically, when dating, women are searching for long-term relationships. Particularly in the '80s, '90s, and early 2000s, almost every TV show and movie had some level of romance in it. Then, celebrity news reporting became obsessed with celebrity dating. Our music speaks also about finding love. Constantly reinforcing these notions of love, makes us desperate for love. Often in relationships, many women return to being the little girl watching Cinderella waiting to be rescued to live happily ever after.

Men, on the other hand, have been conditioned to hunt and conquer. Those skills are introduced to boys at a young age. He-man, Superman, Batman, and Black Panther all were focused primarily on victories and romance was merely a by-product. As a consequence, for some men, when dating there is a desire to accomplish something; perhaps it is to fill their time, have sex, find a wife, rule out who is not their wife, turn someone out, etc.

In an emotional health survey, a random selection of women mentioned that during their teenage years, they were heavily attracted to boys. They were seeking to be loved and wanted to be in a relationship with these young men.[1] Some also said they were seeking validation. Sometimes, for teen girls, gaining the attraction of boys ignites a sense of perceived value if not found in other areas.

Many of us came from homes in which we did not feel loved during the adolescent years. It doesn't mean we weren't loved but we didn't always feel it. Because of that, we may have searched for love in other areas and that also causes us to show up as clingy and needy in romantic relationships.

I was one of those teens who did not feel comfortable at home. Being raised by a clan of "I'm not one of your little friends", "I don't have McDonald's money", and "stop crying or I will give you something to cry about" alpha moms causes us to feel criticized, judged, and misunderstood. Don't get me wrong, they loved us, but their love was hard and often toxic, to be quite frank. I'm just saying.

This type of parenting caused me to pull away. I turned my attention towards friendships and the attention gained from potential suitors because that's where I was able to find a sense of joy and belonging. This is why peer pressure becomes easy to succumb to because the desire to fit in and remain connected to social groups becomes more important than following the guidance of parents that you may not feel understand you. As a teen, I wish I had something in my life that I found more valuable than dating and friendships. I needed to understand that everything I was being told to do (make good grades, obey laws, behave ethically, practice abstinence, etc) was not only leading to being a productive citizen but the fulfillment of a greater purpose.

Nevertheless, If you have spent time with any teen male regardless of whether it's your cousin, brother, son, or nephew, you fully understand that for most, there is nothing that feeds their ego more than a young woman who has a romantic interest in them. This is often the validation that young men are searching for in their social sphere. Now if that young lady is seeking intimacy that is even more of a bonus for them. So young men tap into their desire to conquer and seek these women out just as a tiger searches for their prey in the middle of the night. Their intent is not to cause harm to these young women but to feed their own ego and emotional needs. Harm, however, becomes a side effect.

Because feeding the ego as well as the satisfaction gained from conquering prey can be so addictive, it may cause young men to constantly seek this type of attention, similar to Quentin who was discussed in the introduction. They want more and more of it. Some boys move from feeding the ego to using sex as a tool to mask pain and negative emotions just as drugs and alcohol can do the same. This is how our society develops men with hearty sexual appetites and sex addictions. Please understand that sex addiction doesn't only mean hopping from partner to partner. It can also mean constantly wanting sex from the same partner to the point that it is no longer about pleasure and intimacy with that partner but only about self-gratification. Recently we have seen what happens when sex addictions go untamed— R. Kelly, Bill Cosby, Jeffrey Epstein, and Harvey Weinstein.

Fellas, we need to be honest with ourselves and realize that how we condition men, particularly Black men in this country, robs us of joy and happiness. In late 2020, we interviewed ten Black men to discuss dating, sex, and emotional wounds. Most of these men told us they learned about women and sex from their older brothers, uncles, friends, or older men in the neighborhood that they referred to as "the old heads". From this, they learned very early on about how to please a woman sexually as well as how to get their sexual desires fulfilled. They were often challenged by these men to have as much sex with as many women as possible, equating this behavior to manhood. "How many have you hit yet?" They would ask, "You got you some a$% yet?" This is not only how we continue to further develop men with insatiable sexual appetites but also men who perceive women as objects to conquer[2].

Let's be honest here. Many of us can name at least three Black men who are or were unmarried and under the age of eighteen with a child. Many of us can name a Black man who has multiple children by multiple women.

Just as we have conditioned women to believe sex is the only way to achieve intimacy, we have raised men who value sexual pleasure over self-discipline.

Society has told men to sow their oats. So excessively they sex and date until they are ready to settle down. This process breads men who can be so emotionally damaged from the sowing of oats that they become difficult to live with.

I was listening to a sermon preached by Dr. Matthew Stevenson. In this sermon, he illustrated that after a few months of being married to his beautiful wife, Kamiliah, they disagreed. In a bout of anger, he said to her, "If I'm so mean, why are you always in my pocket?" Now his wife was a woman who had come from a wealthy family and had her own identity, education, and finances upon entering the marriage. For Dr. Stevenson, he spent many years serial dating the wrong women, so he did not know how to treat his God-given Queen.[3] In that moment of anger, his brokenness rose to the surface. This is an example of how we develop emotionally damaged men with stunted emotional intelligence regarding relationships.

Other times, men become so accustomed to the dating life that they find it a challenge to find one woman to meet their needs. They miss the variety offered by having multiple partners.

Our music plays a part in this experience as well. I adore hip hop, rap, and R&B and believe that it is a true form of artistic expression. I also recognize that many of the lyrics are hyper-sexualized and focus on men feeding their sexual appetites with multiple women. For many years, young Black men have acted out on this behavior.

In October of 1982, Marvin Gaye wrote and sang in the hit Motown produced song "Sexual Healing."
"Helps to relieve my mind
Sexual healing, baby, is good for me."

Years later, in January of 1989, the infamous rap group 2 Live Crew produced and sang "Me So Horny." Some of the controversial lyrics written by Luther Campbell stated:
"I'm like a dog in heat, a freak without warnin'
I have an appetite for sex, 'cause me so horny."

In July of 2001, Ludacris and Nate Dogg sang the lyrics written by Fred Tatlow and others, "I've got hoes in different area codes."

More recently, in August of 2018, Travis Scott said in the song produced by Hit-boy "Sicko Mode" from the album *Astro World*:
"All of these hoes I made off records I produced
I might take all my exes and put 'em all in a group."

Meanwhile, our white counterparts, such as Creed, mentions prayer in the song "With Arms Wide Open."[4]

The ballad sung by Maroon 5, "She Will Be Loved" states:
"Beauty queen of only eighteen
She had some trouble with herself
He was always there to help her."[5]

We have created a society in which men equate sex with success and view women as merely an extension of that. There are indeed many men who believe the more popular and wealthier you are the more women you should be smashing. Many women believe that the more wealthier and powerful a man is, the more interesting he becomes. They become more competitive as they compete for his attention. The late rapper Christopher Wallace AKA the Notorious Biggie Smalls had an estimated net worth of almost 10 million upon his death in 1997.[6] During the highlight of his career, three very attractive women were amongst the many who were competing for his attention although in his lyrics he stated, "black and ugly as ever however..."[7,8]

This also causes men to make self-gratification their primary focal point and is the reason some men will have sex without protection. They may find it difficult to keep their desires at bay. The addiction of lust gains control causing them to engage in very risky behavior. This is how we duplicate the cycle of dysfunctional relationships as well as broken homes.

Black women, we must also realize that we have bought into this.

Foxy Brown sang a song about her "Ill Na Na" and we all knew what that stood for.[9]

Rihanna proclaimed, "Sex with me is amazing."[10]

And today Cardi B says, "I don't cook, I don't clean, let me tell you how I got this ring."[11]

We mislead women with these lyrics into believing that we can sex a man into relationships or marriage. When that fails, we take what we believe is the next step and that is having a child by him to keep him in our lives hoping this will bring him to commitment.

One thing we cannot deny is the power of music. The language of emotions, music has the power to control us. Consider how you feel when you hear your favorite song. Think about how easy it is to remember the lyrics to songs but how difficult it is to remember your favorite poem, historical date, or Bible verse. Think about a scene in a movie and the music or score that played in the background. I'm sure it made you feel the moment intensely. This is how powerful music is. It transcends our soul and rides a wave right into our emotions taking over our thoughts and feelings. And our thoughts soon become actions.

I also believe that some of this is a product of the legacy that was passed down to us from our ancestors. For the enslaved who had no rights, sex became one of the very few pleasures they were allowed to enjoy on the plantation. Sexuality became the more intensified part of our ancestors' lives which morphed us into very sensual and passionate beings. This is one of the reasons we write the love songs that are the bangers.

Additionally, Black men were breeders during slavery. They were used to impregnate women slaves to produce children that would be raised to become slaves. However, hundreds of years later, many of us are still stuck in this belief that sex is the primary source of pleasure for us. So we surrender to the lust and the toxic relationships hoping they will make us whole yet instead they steal our joy.

There is nothing more traumatizing than a woman who loves a man but he uses her for sex. Let me be perfectly honest and tell you that many women who you see today are wounded because of this very experience. It could have happened many years ago but the scars are still very present.

My grandmother would always say to me, "Having sex before marriage is a sin and God will not like it." I believed God and my grandmother were both haters who were trying to prevent me from having a good time. As I grew older (much older), I began to research to understand sex. The information was priceless and something I wish I understood much earlier on.

Here's the thing:

The cerebral cortex is the gray matter that makes up the outer layer of the brain. It's the part of your brain that's responsible for higher functions like planning and thinking. This includes thinking about sex.

"A key hormone released during sex is oxytocin. This lowers our defenses and makes us trust people more," says Dr Arun Ghosh, a GP specializing in sexual health at the Spire Liverpool Hospital[12]. This is why people say love is blind.

Oxytocin is also the key to bonding because it increases levels of empathy. But here is the trick, women produce far more of this hormone than men. In addition, our bodies can't distinguish whether the person we're with is a one-night stand, casual fling, or marriage material — oxytocin is released either way.[12]

Men, on the other hand, instead of getting a surge of oxytocin for bonding, receive a gush of a pleasure chemical called dopamine. And as Dr. Ghosh says, "this surge can be addictive".[12] So after I read this, I realized that God and my grandma were not haters. Instead, they wanted the best for me. God, particularly, understood how our bodies work and was trying to prevent me from heartache.

But here is another factor to consider—what I call the mac and cheese effect. The ability to make macaroni and cheese is a badge of honor in the Black community. I make a pretty darn good macaroni and cheese myself. Recall the first time you tasted macaroni and cheese. Perhaps your grandmother or mother made it. Quite possibly they had their particular way of sprucing it up as most do. Perhaps they added sour cream, condensed milk, or a blend of various types of cheeses they shredded by hand. Maybe they went heavy on the salt. Whatever they did you enjoyed it and it set the bar for how you preferred your macaroni and cheese. You visit a friend for dinner and macaroni and cheese happens to be on the menu. As you take your first bite, you can tell immediately that it has been prepared differently than the one you grew accustomed to eating. You may enjoy it but not nearly as much as you enjoy your initial bite. Every bite you take you compare it to the mac and cheese that is so beloved. You miss the flavor and the combination of the ingredients that you typically eat.

This can sometimes be a similar attitude towards sex and relationships. Your first encounter or the first to have your heart sets the tone. And everyone after you subconsciously compare to him/her even if it's in very subtle ways. This is the essence of soul ties because this person has left a lasting imprint on your soul. No one should have to compete with your past.

How many of us engaged in therapy after our first heartbreak or failed relationship? I certainly didn't. However, looking back over my life, I certainly wish I did. I noticed that I projected lots of feelings, fears, and insecurities onto the next. I brought all of the toxic tools I gained from that relationship into the next.

Our society as a whole has a culture of serial dating and casual sex that causes us to jump from one bed to another without hesitation and from one relationship to another. I often used a new love interest as a means to get over the pain from a break-up. Today, I can see that this behavior made for a damaged, less-than-whole version of myself. Had I gone to therapy after a breakup, I would have been able to delve into why these relationships meant so much to me and the feelings these breakups were bringing to the surface.

Our Society has become so sex-seduced that we jump onto any trends that fill our passions and sexual appetites. This trend of serial dating and casual hook-ups was caused by the media. The media is powerful in that whatever is shown in our society blindly follows and it becomes a trend. It was sometime during the late 90s when the HBO TV show *Sex and the City* aired. This beloved show featured four stylish women living in Manhattan drinking cosmopolitans and martinis while discussing their romantic life over Sunday brunch.[13] Because of this show Sunday brunch, colorful martinis, and cosmos became very popular. That's the power of the media.

The media shows us that engaging in a bunch of casual sex is fine and we not only accept it but run with it because it looks appealing. Television shows depict casual sex and people having sex without thought. When you don't know your identity it's easy to follow the trends. We must be careful because everything put in front of us isn't good for us. Particularly when it comes to the things we see in the media. We must realize that the media isn't operated by individuals with degrees in psychology or those who study human behavior. Therefore, they aren't capable of dictating what is good for us.

In many other cultures, men are reared to marry. They are fully explained the benefits of marriage. This is the example that is put in front of them. Their fathers are married, their grandfathers are married, and they are encouraged to marry. Why? Because marriage is the basis for building strong families and wealth. The Institutes for Family Studies states,

"Stats prove that established married men and women have more than $640,000 in assets, while the remarried have more than $450,000 in assets. By contrast, divorced and never married Americans have only about $167,000 in assets when they reach pre-retirement years."[14] I find it perplexing that the conversations within our community regarding building wealth do not encourage our men to marry. Wealth is just one of the many benefits of marriage.

Now before y'all email me, I want to be clear that I understand that marriage isn't everyone's goal and it certainly doesn't have to be but I do want to share that there are marriage benefits.

A key point that I want to make is that there is no place in the Bible that God condemns consensual sex. Sex is beautiful and he created it to unite married couples together. Sex is more than just a good feeling; it bonds you and changes you. Don't believe me, read the Song of Solomon in the Bible. It's all about Solomon having hot sex with his wife.

"Blow on my garden that its fragrance may spread abroad. Let my lover come into his garden and taste its choice fruits."[15]

I love this book of the Bible because not only is it about sex but about intimacy and that is the better part of sex. It's like the icing on the cake. He wants us to use sex responsibly and in a way that maintains our emotional health as well as the emotional health of our romantic partners. God is our father and as His children, He isn't giving us rules necessarily but loving guidance and protection. The choices we make are up to us to decide.

The issue is that we do not encourage self-regulation and self-control in our community. Self-control stops us from having children before we are prepared, self-control prevents us from spending our finances poorly, it prevents us from getting so drunk that we make poor decisions, and from giving everyone a piece of our mind. We can't control anything else in life if we don't have control of ourselves. It is often because of unhealed emotional wounds that we overindulge in sex and other things.

Several years ago, I worked with a woman that I call Cru. She was tall, perhaps about 5'9 with honey brown skin. She had a beautiful face and a tiny waist. She had a Double D-sized chest and a big booty to match it. Cru was rather quiet and always had a solemn look on her face as if she found everything on earth to be uninteresting. She was never the type of girl who caused a bunch of commotion but was focused on working to pay her bills.

Now on the other hand Caswell was a tall dark-skinned brother from the islands. He had silky smooth dark chocolate skin. It was the kind of skin that glowed flawlessly. He was without higher education but he had a quick wit and a way with words. He was confident not in an arrogant manner but in a way that made you believe that he knew what he was talking about and whenever he spoke everyone listened. This brother could sell termites to a homeowner and make them believe they needed them.

He always had a connection to everything. If a new club was opening in the city, Caswell could get you on the list. If there was a big party, Caswell would have a table with full bottle service –for free, Honey!

Along the way, he developed a keen interest in Cru that quickly developed into uncontrollable lust. He would be in the middle of a conversation but if she walked by he would stop mid-sentence to stare at her. During meetings, he could always be found glancing at Cru out of his peripheral vision. Gifts for her and small trinkets would be left on her desk almost daily. He love-bombed her while lusting for her something terrible and everyone in the office knew about it. Every conversation with him regardless of whether it was about a work-related spreadsheet, football, or the weather would always lead back to her. If she was in the lunchroom having her lunch you could count on him to be somewhere very close by hoping to catch a glimpse of her.

One evening, we had an office happy hour at a nearby lounge. On that night, Caswell purchased a room at the Four Seasons in Georgetown for her along with a nice dinner via room service. Even the cheapest room at the Four Seasons was easily 750 per night. I watched the two of them hop into an Uber together and ride off into the night. To this day, I'm not exactly sure what happened that night but she was found in the early morning hours bloodied and with a face full of tears.

In the following days, there were many different stories and rumors that would come from that night. It was almost as if it was an episode of Dateline NBC. Some say she changed her mind but he refused to hear it and forced himself on her. Others say he got rough with her when she refused to do the things he asked. It was so bad that it became a human resources issue, the police were involved, and he was put on suspension without pay.

The two of them never spoke to each other again while Cru was left to deal with the remnants— emotional wounds from the betrayal and a professional image that was now in question. This experience left her with the fear of being disrespected by a man.

Cru also began to notice the stares she was now receiving from colleagues. She was aware of the judgments that pointed to the abuse being her fault for being deemed a tease or for spending alone time with him. "She put herself in that situation," was what many men and women chalked it up to. "I don't want her on this particular project, she is drama," is what another male colleague stated to me as we were resource planning.

This type of situation is not an anomaly. I've heard from many women including friends who were assaulted by men who could not handle a change of mind or dealt with men who handled them roughly.

I've also heard from women who were forced into having sex from men whom they thought were friends during what they believed were innocent encounters. These types of situations diminish the ability of women to trust men.

In addition to the lack of ability to regulate, including listening endlessly to music referring to women as broads, hoes, dimes, dames, hotties, bitches, work, or anything other than human, causes men to view women as objects instead of beings with hearts and feelings. The respect and honor for women is lost in these types of lyrics and drives a culture of men who are just looking for the next smash by any means necessary.

After the incident, during a staff meeting, I brushed past Cru as she walked in and took a seat. Suddenly, I saw Caswell point to Cru turn to a male colleague, and, out of his damaged emotions and wounded ego, whisper, "Do you want to tap that? I'm finished with it."

There are many women, quite like Cru and myself, who have experienced this level of disrespect from men by being thought of as if we are mere objects to be used. There is nothing more sickening than seeing a man disrespect a woman by cursing them out, threatening them, or putting them through any other form of humiliation because they did not adhere to their advances or give them the attention they desired. Women shouldn't be expected to sacrifice our souls for the pleasure of men while they remove our dignity. It shouldn't be about teaching women to think like a man instead it should be about teaching men to be better human beings.

I love food. If you know me in real life you know how much food means to me. I love all of the bad food– cakes, pies, bread, pasta, french fries. I've gained some weight and my LDL– the bad cholesterol level, has increased because of my diet. Oh, how I wish I could eat whatever I want to eat whenever I want to eat it without pause. I have to regulate myself or else it could make for health problems. So it is with lust and sex. Casual sex is a part of our culture, however, it's not healthy for us. In the movies and our music, we see and hear of people having lots of casual sex, and that has spilled over into our culture. Yet they rarely depict the aftermath which can be soul-compromising and lead us to unhealed emotional wounds.

Questions for Reflection

1. Did you see a therapist after your first breakup and/or first sexual experience? Looking back, do you think it would have been helpful?

2. Consider your views on sex. Have they always been healthy? Describe how your views on sex may have been harmful to you and others.

Activity

Define love, in your own terms. List several characteristics of love. If you are in a romantic relationship, ask your partner to share the answers to the same questions. Do your definitions match?

Chapter 7

The Wounds of Abuse

"Childhood should be carefree, playing in the sun; not living a nightmare in the darkness of the soul."
— **Dave Pelzer,** *A Child Called "It"*

Nijiama

My younger cousin John was eleven years old
when his mother sent him to live with his father and
stepmother in another state. John was an active boy
with a huge imagination and lots of energy. He often
found himself in some form of mischief in and
outside of school. His kryptonite, however, was that
he could not control his impulses which would cause
him to say things that he did not mean to say. For
him, it was as if the words would fly out of his mouth
before he was able to catch them or consider the
consequences. He did many things without thought
such as locking his younger cousin in a closet that
often landed him in quite a bit of trouble. His
stepmother didn't believe in testing, diagnoses, and
disorders being responsible for his behavior. She
believed he was a "bad kid" and that stiff punishment
and stern correction were the answer. "He just needs
to spend about two months with us. I will set him
straight," his stepmother would say. Those comments
were filled with so much pride and arrogance as if she
was the only one that held the key to his discipline
and success. To others, her words came across as if
she was a better parent than most.

From then on, John's days and nights were filled
with lots of reprimanding, delegating, scoffing, and
spankings. During one heated argument between John
and his stepmother, things grew so intense that she
slapped him. Instinctively, John shoved her. As you

can imagine, this made his stepmother furious. Immediately following this incident, she convinced his father that John needed to be sent to a juvenile detention center. On his twelfth birthday, John was dropped off at the facility where he remained for eleven months.

While at the detention facility, John experienced a wave of emotions while he struggled to understand his fate– rejection, sadness, loneliness, and inferiority were the emotions that John had to make space for. He was away from his loved ones while being monitored having his every move regulated. The facility pumped him full of antipsychotic drugs that would turn even the strongest adult into a zombie or make them suicidal. He was abused and his needs were neglected. When he finally was able to leave the facility, John was filled with anger. That situation changed the entire trajectory of his life.

During the teenage years, the brain's prefrontal cortex, the area responsible for decision-making and controlled impulses, is still developing. If a person experiences any incident that their brain codes as trauma during these years and this includes abuse in all forms (ie sexual abuse, heavy alcoholic drinking, indulging in illicit drug usage) this may prohibit the development of that part of the brain. It is for this reason that we have adults who have difficulty performing higher-level thinking such as making and remaining committed to long-term plans and controlling impulses.

Believe it or not, controlling anger and impulses is a very high-level skill. As in John's case, today he is a thirty-something-year-old male who finds it difficult to live a productive life. It is a challenge for him to maintain relationships and control his anger and impulses. Because of many mistakes, finding his value in street life has led him to develop a relationship with the criminal justice system that has resulted in several previous incarcerations.

The book, *The Body Keeps The Score* states, "Trauma impacts the imagination. Fantasies about the future, travel, and food are now inhibited."[1] For this reason, living day by day tends to be the norm for those who suffer from adolescent trauma instead.

For my younger cousin, the pain and agony of that traumatic situation kept him bound and engulfed in shame and guilt. It has caused him to feel inferior so he uses illicit drugs to give him the illusion of superiority and confidence. The drugs also help him to suppress social anxiety. Both sex and drugs help him numb the pain of the memories, flashbacks, and nightmares. Most of our family simply assume that his life is a product of a series of bad choices which is true but they are unaware of what is causing the bad choices. There is always a root cause.

It is difficult for us to talk about our past traumas and to admit when we are victims of abuse. It relates to having healthy conversations about abuse and sex within our families. If those conversations are not being had, the subject becomes taboo and we assume that something is shameful about it and do not speak about it.

This is particularly true for those suffering from sexual-based trauma. What holds us back from mentioning it is our worst fear causing us to question– will they believe me? Will it cause further tension? Will they say it was my fault? Will they view me differently? We often second-guess our memory– perhaps I am recalling this incorrectly. So, we hold on to it. We internalize it, making it a part of us allowing it to skew our views and the way that we interact with people. We feed it with bad choices and allow it to chip away at our wholeness.

When we become traumatized at a very early age, we are forever changed. We are left with a soul that mourns. We are left to figure out how to cope with the emotional pain. Often, rage, addictions, abuse, and bad decisions become the Tylenol of choice.

In our survey, 67% of Black Americans stated they had experienced some form of sexual trauma. What was even more jarring was that of those who admitted they had experienced sexual trauma 83% mentioned they were never able to share the trauma with their parents or caregivers.[2] This tells us that many people are walking amongst us today (friends, family members, colleagues, leaders, etc.) who are living with this type of traumatic secret engulfed in a blanket of shame and pain. This is why we must keep the dialogue open regarding sex so that our children can feel comfortable with sharing their concerns, fears, and pains. As parents, the more intellectually advanced beings, we must be proactive in opening the dialogue instead of running away from it.

In our home, we have removed the sting from sex. Shamon and I do not run when the topic is mentioned or cringe when our children have questions. Our children understand that sex is part of life and that mommy and daddy engage in it regularly. We answer

all questions regarding sex and they understand fully
what it is and how it works. We also make sure they
are fully educated about abstinence, birth control, and
more. I understand that we want to protect our
children and maintain their innocence but in this day
and with so much knowledge being just a swipe away
these conversations are necessary. We cannot allow
peers and the media to raise our children.

Shamon

There are signs all around us. Those directed to our destination. Signs letting us know when it's time to stop. Signs to let us know where we can grab a bite to eat. Even signs that our bodies tell us that something is wrong.

One of the most invaluable signs that I've learned in life is the word stop. Not because someone told me I needed to do it, but it was one that I had to master telling myself.

When I was younger, I would constantly compare myself to others. Did they have the look or the swag and I didn't? Did they have the money and I didn't? Did they have the love and I didn't? But, as clear as a parent talking to a child, this is the word God spoke to me. He said, "STOP!" It wasn't until I paused and internalized that word stop, did I gain astoundment at the abuse it was causing me – it was abuse exacted upon my psyche, my spirit, and my general health.

Up until that moment, I inherently felt like I was the outcast, the person who, when they entered, brought the energy down in the room. I blamed myself for the divorce of my parents. I blamed myself for our family's financial woes. I blamed myself for not having my thoughts, words, and actions all neatly packaged and put together.

Abuse is normally looked at outwardly.

Abuse comes in many forms, but some of the worst is that which we inflict upon ourselves.

Embrace your destiny, not a bad history

Left unchecked Anger and Pride cause temporary to permanent blindness

Question for Reflection

1. Describe instances in which you may have inflicted abuse upon yourself.

Activity
If you have been the victim of abuse, severe trauma, or self-abuse please visit a therapist. Go to www.theblackgirlsguidetohealinemotionalwounds.com to find a directory of therapists to select.

Chapter 8

Identity-ish

"For this purpose, I was born and for this purpose, I have come into the world."
John 18:37

Nijiama

Curtis Carroll was once a kid raised on the streets of east Oakland, CA. He was raised by a single mother and grandmother who were both addicted to crack cocaine. Because of an overcrowded underfunded school system that ruled with an iron fist instead of empathy, Carroll did not learn to read. Frustrated, he dropped out of school and turned to a life of crime to survive. At the young age of seventeen years, he committed murder in a robbery attempt and served almost three decades in San Quentin State Prison.[1]

While in prison, he built a relationship with Jesus Christ, found support, learned to read and write, and began reading the newspaper daily with his particular interest being the financial section. That is where he learned to read and predict the stock market. Today, he is nicknamed the Oracle of San Quentin or simply "Wall Street". He has teamed with Zach Williams, son of the late great Robin Williams, a Columbia University grad to teach financial literacy classes. Caroll is a TEDx speaker and has been featured in numerous documentaries and news outlets including *NPR, Inc.*, *CBS News*, *Market Watch*, *CNN*, and *Black Enterprise* to name a few. He has inspired many families to start investing and has been hailed a financial genius. And here you are today reading about him. This is what makes Black America so fascinating because captivity has never been able to stop us.

During Carroll's teen years, he allowed the school system to tell him who he was. They moved him away from other students to special education classes where he was made to feel different and isolated. They assigned him poor grades D, F thus telling him he is below average and a failure. And these identity wounds had a tremendous impact on him. Children are taught very early on that you go to school— that is your job and your purpose, if you will, at that time. Adults often ask kids, Do you get good grades? But when they are unable to find success in that area and do not have the proper support system it chips away at their self-esteem.

In his TedX talk Mr. Carroll states,

"I committed my first crime at fourteen years old and it was the first time someone told me that I had potential–the first time someone believed in me. Nobody told me I could be a doctor, lawyer, or engineer. So, I thought crime was my way to go."[2]

For Carroll, out of low self-worth and desperation, he turned to what he believed he could do and things that were accessible to him, which was street gang life. That's where he found identity and community.

See the issue is when we do not know our identity, we create room for others to tell us who we are or we change it up to appease others and fit in. We turn to whoever and whatever is accessible to us to determine our identity i.e. groups, religions, ideas, peers, and celebrities who dictate our actions. We see this all the time on social media–

Look at me, I am in this social group. This is how I must behave now. I am someone. I'm valuable.

I'm wearing designer clothes that show you I am rich and important.

Shamon always says, "Children should be read and not written." Imagine how different life would have been if Carroll's community had helped him to understand who he was and to bring out the intellect inside of him. Imagine how different your life could be if you fully understood what was inside of you. Yet instead we allow everyone else to tell us who and what we should be. We allow our music to tell us to sell drugs, hustle and have multiple women. We allow the older damaged men in our lives to tell us to conquer as many women as possible. We allow celebrities and Instagram models to tell us what to wear and how to behave instead of fully understanding what is inside of ourselves.

Dr. Myles Munroe made a powerful statement during a seminar, "Each of us comes to earth but you determine how much of you is manifested once you are here."[3] When God released us into this earth, he filled us with all of the things we need to be successful. However, we become tainted by everyone dictating to us who and what we are. We have to determine who we are and what is inside of us – whether it's extending compassion, a knack for translating complex information like Mr. Carroll, negotiation, making people feel welcome, or other abilities it's up to us individually to do the work to determine our gifts. But we have to understand who we are and frame our identity on that.

Lack of identity also causes us to form unhealthy attachments to things. We have all known Jared as mentioned in the introduction or someone like him. Jared has been for many of us our brother, our cousin, or maybe our husband. For us ladies, he may have been the guy we have dated. For the guys that are reading perhaps you see some of the characteristics and traits in your behavior. Jared is what happens when we are searching for identity. Lack of identity causes us to build unhealthy attachments to things because we are looking for them to make us great. We are looking for Gucci, BMW, and LV to make us great when we should be searching for greatness within ourselves. The Bible tells us that God promised to make "our name great" yet here we are posting pics of ourselves in designer clothes and cars recalibrating the algorithms to make these products trend which will continue to make these designers great.

Our identity should be established upon four very important questions:

1. Who am I?
2. Whose am I?
3. What do I stand for (values)?
4. Why am I here?

If you ever listen to any of Mr. Carroll's many interviews you will hear the answers to these questions and you will see these answers are upon which his life is now built. Hardly ever bragging, rather he starts each interview by sharing his humble life beginnings and then goes into his relationship with Jesus Christ which has helped him to answer, "whose am I?"

Often he states, "I am made to do this," as he talks about the work he does to educate people in and outside of the criminal justice system on finances.[2] I have never heard anyone make stocks, wealth, and finances (subjects I find boring and mundane) sound so appealing. He speaks with an abundance of knowledge (as if he has a photographic memory), enthusiasm, and charisma.

He also speaks about what he stands for or his values. One value he takes pride in is walking in integrity. He speaks heavily about how important this is for him at this stage in his life.

Shaping his life around solid values has moved him from a statistic destined for a life behind bars to a worldwide success. When people encounter him, their lives are better than before they met him. That's the result of knowing your identity which leads to purpose. Let me tell you there is no greater joy than fulfilling your God-given purpose.

A bonus to understanding our identity is it causes us to no longer live in the comparison trap. Knowing who we are means understanding how we are wired and the niche that makes us unique. Consequently, we become so in tune with ourselves and grateful for our abilities and skills that comparing ourselves to others is irrelevant and a waste of our time. We can see and appreciate the talents of others but remain overwhelmed by the gifts God endowed us with. Knowing our identity and appreciating how God intricately and specifically made us causes jealousy, envy, and discontentment to stand back!

****

As I was scrolling through social media, I saw the trailer for the anticipated Netflix Show *The Light We Carry* featuring Oprah Winfrey as she interviewed the former First Lady Michelle Obama. I'd been anticipating its release because reading the book brought me so much joy. I glanced through the comments hoping to see the excitement of others regarding the series. Instead of excitement, the comments I saw were mean and nasty. These comments, written by adult professional women and men, were filled with child-like name-calling, featurism attacks, and racially charged teasing of the former First Lady.

What I found mind-boggling about this is that Mrs. Obama is a woman born and raised on American soil and reared on the Southside of Chicago. She worked very hard to graduate from two of the most prestigious universities on the globe which only a very small percentage gained acceptance to and became a lawyer and a Dean at the University of Chicago. Every book she has written and every platform she has held has been about positive change. She represents every bit of the American dream that this country has become famous for. However, none of these keyboard thugs saw that. All they saw was a Black woman who looked different from them sitting in seats that were not designed for her and that bothered them. It's not simply about when they see us, it's also how they see us.

Fortunately, Mrs. Obama has not been moved by the vile comments. She is truly the picture of grace under fire. She is accustomed to sexism, racism, and being seen by only racial stereotypes in various forms. During her tenure at Princeton University, the mother of her white roommate attempted to get her daughter's room reassigned because of Lady Obama's race.[4] Boy, I'd give anything to see how the two of them feel about that decision now. Yet, there is a part of me that believes that family still has no regrets.

One of the things that Mrs. Obama accounts for her success is her family. She came from a very close-knit clan that included her parents who were very supportive, nurturing, and empowering. In her books, she speaks about major events held by her family to celebrate special occasions and accomplishments. These events were attended by cousins, uncles, and aunts. In this, she found safety and support along with the courage to be herself.[4] This is the power that comes from being raised in a strong family– identity.

As for Black America as a whole, because our ancestors had to leave behind their culture through the diaspora, we lost much of our original identity. Today, we are still searching for our collective identity moving from one paradigm to another clutching on to any belief, religion, or ideology that we think will explain who we are and why we are here. Yet these things only leave us empty.

One of the aspects that makes it a challenge for us to show up as our authentic selves is that we believe those outside of our race do not see nor appreciate our originality. They see what they have been raised to see by their elders or what the media has conditioned them to see and often it's negative. And to some degree, I believe we have bought into this as well.

On one hot summer day, when I was about six years old my family purchased watermelon for my cousins and me to eat. We knew the watermelon was sticky, so we took it outside. When my mother saw us eating the watermelon on the front lawn, frantically she ran to bring us back inside. As kids, we were confused and thought, "What did we do wrong?' My mother explained that we should never allow white people to see us eating watermelon because it contributed to the stereotype of poor Blacks eating watermelon.

I also remember a time as a young professional fresh out of college, I was late for a meeting. As I entered the room, I sat beside one of my Black colleagues and she whispered to me, "Don't be late for meetings especially when White people are attending the meeting. It's not a good look." Who else has been subjected to thinking such as this?

This type of rhetoric gives us a burden instead of freedom because it forces us to concern ourselves with the perceptions of others that we cannot control instead of the role we came to perform. We have become consumed with being what others want us to be so they can feel safe with us even at the expense of our identity.

Would you believe me if I told you that this hasn't always been the case? Allow me to take you back to the late '60s and the '70s. During this time as we were united and fighting for our rights there was a strong feeling of Black pride in the air. This was just after the Civil Rights Movement and revolutionaries were rising denouncing everything we, as Black Americans, were conditioned to believe while giving us a paradigm shift in thinking—Angela Davis, Assatu Shakur, and Stokely Carmichael were changing the community along with our ideals about race while screaming Black power. During this time, we released the terms "negro" and "colored people" and began referring to ourselves as Black— the identity we chose. We also began showing the world our natural hair by wearing big kinky afros and braids with beads as James Brown sang, "I'm Black and I'm proud." Our children were given beautiful African names such as Aesa, Kwame, Kadida, and Zane which all had meaning and origination. We made statements such as "the blacker the berry, the sweeter the juice", and "black don't crack." We were waving our fists in the air as we enjoyed our Blackness and culture. But, towards the end of the 1970s, as we began to embrace assimilation, somewhere along the way, we lost that feeling.

One of the things Baby boomers and Gen Xers are known for is wanting to climb the corporate ladder. I'm a member of Gen X and I believe we felt that to embrace the corporate climb we had to release our culture. We stopped believing in our communities, our culture, and ourselves as we wrapped our arms around assimilation. We focused heavily on fitting in. We traded our authenticity for acceptance as we cut our afros, relaxed our hair, and referred to things that represent Black culture as "ghetto". If I must be honest, I have done this myself. It's the thing inside of us that makes us remove our braids before going on the job interview or cutting out the locks before we start the job. It's the thing inside of us that causes us to remove our African name from the resume out of fear of not gaining the opportunity. It's what causes us to look down on a colleague for wearing her big kinky, curly 'fro or ethnic hairstyle to the conference. It's the thoughts that make us question ourselves constantly when we are standing next to our white colleagues–

Do I sound too aggressive?
Did I use slang when I spoke?
Are my clothes too bright or fitted?
Are they comfortable with my new hairstyle?

It's the desire to make our counterparts feel comfortable with us. Let's be honest with ourselves. What is the message we are trying to send when we do these things? Perhaps we do it because we genuinely want to increase our chances of obtaining the opportunity. After all, we know that people do discriminate against these factors. But let's dig deeper; we may be aiming to send a message that says, "I'm a good Black person, you can let your guard down around me, you can trust me, I'm not like the others."

Not only did we want to be accepted, but we also wanted to fit our white counterparts' brand of professionalism because, let's face it, they created the narrative of professionalism and attached the definition to it. We have often heard the term, "not a fit" or "not a cultural fit" in professional settings. I believe this vague term was created to keep people out who did not meet what was defined as the standard of professionalism. So to win, we code-switch and assimilate.

This can be considered a form of unhealed wounds because daily, we are forced to put on a costume. We are forced to deny our being to become something else for the sake of someone else's comfort while neglecting our interests. It looks like having conversations about listening to Pearl Jam, Harry Styles, Taylor Swift, and Maroon 5 knowing that we'd prefer to talk about Cardi B, Beyonce, Future, and SZA. It looks like keeping up with *Gossip Girl* and *Friends* to participate in the office "water-cooler" conversation when we would rather watch *Bel-Aire* and *Power*. It looks like creating fake narratives and memories about our childhood so that others will not look down on us and perceive us as deprived.

Acceptance and identity are very closely related. We all have a natural desire to be accepted in the environments we spend our time and that has the power to shape our identity. Mr. Carroll didn't feel accepted in school yet he found it in street life and that dictated his actions. In professional settings, we do what we can to gain acceptance even if it compromises our identity.

Work hurts are emotional wounds and can have a lasting impact on us. This is why it's essential for us, personally, to remain surrounded by people who love us and appreciate the real us, particularly during our formative years. This builds our self-esteem and helps us to remain unbreakable and immovable in all types of environments even when others can't see past stereotypes.

Shamon

One day, when I was a preteen, I was walking back to school after having lunch at McDonald's with friends. I was attacked by a group of guys who saw us as easy targets who had entered into their turf or neighborhood. These guys were hanging out at the corner and appeared to be on edge and ready to fight or sell their "street pharmaceuticals" to prove to themselves and one another their street cred. As the guys approached us, one accosted my friends and said, "What's in your pockets? It don't matter, I need dat." When I drifted back towards my friend, that's when their attention turned towards me, and before I knew it, the situation escalated quickly because I wouldn't let the group go through my pockets. Out of fear, my friends abandoned me and fled the scene. Then before I knew it, I was amid a scuffle with several guys punching and kicking me.

That incident left me feeling helpless. It took a toll on my self-esteem and confidence. Because of that incident, I only wanted to stay inside the house and never return to school in fear that the incident would happen again. From then, I focused on my studies and learned how to advocate and navigate my way in, through, and out of school with great precision. I spent lots of time reading, researching, and preparing for exams. The fear my mom held of trying to avoid a situation like this by sending me further away to a "good school" versus the neighborhood school backfired. However, this focused, planning time changed. I was later transferred to my neighborhood school and it resulted in me graduating from high school with honors as our class valedictorian.

I have used that incident as a part of my identity – in that I view myself as not only a survivor, I'm also an overcomer! It shook me but didn't break me and that fact alone has improved my self-esteem. I believe there is value in every single situation. I could have died that day or been seriously injured, however God had different plans and a purpose for me and my life.

It can be tough to gain our sense of identity with so many people around telling us who we are and what we should be doing. As kids, particularly in the Black community, often people call us by the name or nickname that they view us as. I can recall hearing a young mother constantly referring to her child as "aggravating". I'm sure that she was partly referring to her child as that in jest however this will have an impact on the type of adult the child becomes. Being referred to by these types of words as children can make us feel small and disempowered. They cause us to grow up looking for ways to remain under the radar and to lose our voice as we want to prevent being annoying.

Today, I listen to my pre-teen daughter as she speaks about her classmates. As she mentions each one she will tell me what group they identify with– Emos, Baddies, and so on. In my younger days, we had groups too. They were either hustlers or Dboys, athletes, aspiring rappers, fighters, pretty boys, or nerds. Fitting into these groups filled us with belonging because we now had a community of people to associate with which is something all beings crave. Additionally, the labels helped to easily explain who we were, and that for a time felt empowering.

As adults, we still try to fit in groups partly because our brains are wired to search for patterns and connections. These patterns bring us comfort and the connections help us make sense of the world as we hear and see perspectives that are similar or identical to our own. But often as children we mislabel others and put them into a box that isn't a fit for them or one they can't get out of.

The biggest question I get asked often is "How did you make it out of the "hood?" According to statistics, I'm supposed to be in prison, illiterate, dead, or have a bunch of children by many different women leaving a trail of broken homes. That was the culture I was raised in and I know many people who unfortunately arrived at that fate. Even though I was raised in a crime-ridden area with lots of social ills, I still had a community. I had many older wise men and women in my life who constantly encouraged me and told me how smart I was and to lean on my intellect and not follow behind others. This is why a healthy family and community are vital to our identity just as much as the air we breathe.

Questions for Reflections

1. If I were to ask your most recent romantic partner, your past boss, and your closest friend to list 3 character traits that describe you, what would each list state?

2. List 3 of your values (what you stand for or beliefs that motivate how you behave toward others).

3. What are you passionate about?

4. Describe a situation in which you toned down your Blackness. How did it make you feel? Why do you believe you found it necessary to do so?

5. Consider 2 or 3 recent public situations you have been in. How did race impact those situations?

Chapter 9

Finance Wounds

"Don't tell me what you value, show me your budget, and I'll tell you what you value."
– Joe Biden

Nijiama

In May of 2020, Maurice Fayne, also known as Arkansas Moe, of VH1 Love and Hip-Hop Atlanta, was arrested and charged with federal bank fraud for misusing funds from the Federal Paycheck Protection Program[1]. During the pandemic stay-at-home order, many businesses, such as restaurants, hair salons, spas, and consulting firms were unable to provide services, resulting in a loss of revenue and income for businesses and workers. Many feared losing their homes and livelihoods.

The Federal Paycheck Protection Program was designed to help these businesses and their employees remain afloat. Allegedly, Arkansas Moe misused the 2.5 million dollar funds that he received on extravagant purchases for himself. He purchased a 5.7 diamond carat ring, a diamond bracelet, and a Rolex watch. Fayne also leased a Rolls Royce.[1] He posted these and other purchases regularly on his Instagram account. This behavior is a clear indication of unhealed emotional wounds.

Our relationship with finances began when we were children. As we socialize with our peers, our awareness develops and we start to pay attention to our differences. For many Black Americans, whether we were born into extreme poverty or the middle class, we recognized that our experiences differed from some of our white counterparts. Let me give you an example; I can recall attending private school and hearing my white classmates discuss their summer trips to cities such as Paris and London. I, on the other hand, spent the summer at grandma's in the hood who was reluctant to turn on the air conditioning because she feared a pricey bill that her fixed income couldn't afford. My peers discussed lake house vacations, spending Saturdays floating on the river on glass-bottom boats, and taking trips to the beach in their private airplanes.

Some of us may have grown up seeing Black peers with name-brand shoes and who could afford professional hair styling or cuts. We had to wear hand-me-downs and go without some of the latest trends.

These things can make us feel isolated and degrade our self-worth because we think—Why not me? Those things that we didn't have access to in our youth become the focal point of our aspirations.

When I was a kid, it seemed like all I heard was adults talking about money problems and what they could do if they acquired a lot of money. The television shows I watched didn't help either. On the *Facts of Life* Blair Warner, the rich blonde who seemed as if she didn't have a care in the world, often spoke of extravagant shopping at Bloomingdales and Neiman Marcus.[2] When Shamon and I got married, one of the first purchases I made was a set of towels from Bloomingdales. As I trailed my fingers along the luxurious cotton of the overpriced towels it was as if I had Blair's financial freedom. It felt like a distant reality had now come true for me. However, this was far from the truth.

As an adult, I realized that my childhood impacted my relationship with money and how I viewed money. I saw money as a savior, as a tool that could solve all problems and could change the way people perceived me. Therefore, I wanted lots of it.

Today, many of us are first generation; we are the first to attend college and beyond, earn high salaries, buy nice homes, and travel outside of the Americas. However, in our hearts, we may be still looking at the world through the lens of poverty. We are still thirsting after things we could not afford as children and that drives the need for more things. We want to show off, floss, flaunt, stunt, front, and impress the world with the most expensive shoes, large houses, fancy cars, and the best vacations. We are quick to tell someone our children attend the priciest private schools and when we've joined the most exclusive group. Why? Because we believe it proves our worth. We want the world to know that we aren't poor, and therefore we have value.

If we grew up poor, we believe that money is the solution to all of our problems because that was where many of our childhood issues stemmed from. So we lust for a windfall–

- *If I could just win the lottery*
- *I wish I could gain a large settlement*
- *I just need to get my hands on *insert any large sum of money* my problems will be over*

And as adults, when we acquire any lump sum of money, we overindulge our senses quite like Arkansas Moe. We buy designer and noticeable name brands. We make grand purchases for our children without educating them on assets over liabilities. This is how the cycle of consumerism and poverty continues to repeat itself. We purchase these things partly because we want to be happy but also because we subconsciously believe it is healing our wounded emotions. We remember the day in our childhood when we didn't have what the other kids had.

How are we triggered by financial wounds? When money gets tight, I get depressed. It causes me to feel helpless and inferior because money was put on such a high pedestal in my family.

It is even more bleaker for single-parent households. Black children in homes headed by single parents are about 3.5 times more likely to live in poverty compared to Black children living with two parents in a first marriage.[3]

My friend Grace grew up in section eight housing. She was born to a single mother who birthed five children by four different fathers. In Grace's home, money was always tight. The landline (and only) phone would be without service for weeks. When I'd go over for a visit, I would hear her mom speaking with her friends about the items the children needed, shoes, school supplies, or winter coats. These conversations often led to long discussions about the fathers not doing their part.

My friend's mother gladly accepted all types of currency from whoever could provide it. She rarely turned anything down from anyone, even if it was from a married man in search of a weekend thrill or a much younger man who was around her eldest daughter's age.

As a teen, my friend Grace often didn't have enough money to go to a movie with friends or to purchase the latest fashions. Sometimes she went to school on an empty stomach, and worried about being evicted because too many people lived in her home breaking the rules of the government subsidy. Frequently, when she needed something her mother responded with, "Call your daddy and ask him for it," knowing he would drop the ball. These events rewired her brain. And as trauma does it can cause us to make irrational decisions.

Because money seemed to be the root of all of her childhood issues, my friend Grace believes that money equates to love. When we were younger, she always dated the drug dealers in town. After that, she pursued professional athletes, accepting all of the emotional abuse and narcissism that can be attached to that lifestyle. Today, she is in a relationship with a man who pays part of her rent however he doesn't make himself available to her. Excuse after excuse he is not present to celebrate her birthday, or major holidays, or to escort her to weddings or special events. His behavior causes quite a bit of tension and friction between the two. She tells us often that she is fed up and plans to leave, but it never happens. He knows there is a wound there he can take advantage of. He pays her bills and tells her loves her, and that keeps her committed.

Curtis Carroll states that the way we spend money is tied to our emotions. "Emotional spending is a direct result of the human need for power, beauty, love, and choice," Carroll states.[4] We must confront the feelings surrounding these needs– and that involves reconciling with the past.

We have to combat our previous toxic notions about money and realize that it isn't our savior but rather a tool. We have to learn to value ourselves more than the opinions of others. That means not shopping to impress or making purchases for social media clout. Instead, let's spend our money on things that will position us for wealth and true success.

Shamon

Coming from an impoverished background may cause us to financially live in the moment. Our brain becomes wired to spend and societal pressures cause our lives to dwindle to prove we have money–that we have finally arrived. Particularly for those who grew up in an environment like mine where saving money wasn't celebrated. We simply didn't have it to save so keeping the lights on became a huge event for us.

It took so much for me to learn (I had to retrain my brain) that money is more than just paying bills and buying lots of fancy things. It's working on a financial plan for ourselves and, if applicable for our family. It's about seeing it as a tool to work for you. When you are awake your focus should be on how to earn money and where to put it; while you are asleep your money should be working for you. Financial instability causes most to feel insecure. When the finances are in order, the man can be at peace.

Questions for Reflection:

1. What was the financial situation of your family during your childhood?

2. How was money perceived by your family during your childhood?

3. How do you view money today?

4. Aside from housing and childcare, what are the top four items you spend most of your money on? Why are these items important to you?

5. Do you find it easy or difficult to save and invest monthly? Why?

6. List 3 ways you can begin to change any unhelpful views you may have regarding money.

Chapter 10

Church Hurt

"The loftiest statement of your cleansing and redemption—after all the pain you've endured—is that now you realize what god was doing and you can get on with that high calling for your life."
— **Stephen Mansfield,** *Healing Your Church Hurt: What To Do When You Still Love God But Have Been Wounded by His People*

Nijiama

With all of its flaws, I love the church, particularly the Black church. Growing up in the Bible Belt, church attendance was a big part of early development. Attending services for most of the day on Sundays and then returning for prayer and Bible study during the week was normal for me.

In my hometown in South Carolina, churches were the centerpieces of the community with membership being tied to the family you were raised in. Churches also were known for hosting community events that we all looked forward to attending. Weekly, my grandmother would search the newspaper to see which churches were hosting events. Friends and Family Days were a huge hit and provided an opportunity to visit other churches. In the summertime, every child looked forward to attending vacation Bible school, and the annual revivals were packed. The bonus for me was after a funeral or major event you can expect to be served a nice warm homestyle meal. And let me tell ya, the ladies that prepared those meals certainly knew exactly what they were doing in the kitchen– crispy fried chicken, tender collards, and the moistest pound cake ever.

Church is a wonderful place but it also at times has represented the worst of who we are. We must admit that there are individuals within the Black church and the Christian church as a whole who misrepresented godly principles. At times, the power of the church has been given away to movements such as the prosperity gospel, Purity Culture, and the notorious faith-cure movement. We have seen pastors and lay leaders controlled by their egos and vices, abuse and damage the very people they were sent to help. We have also seen some mishandle mental illness very poorly by making it a faith issue instead of one that is therapeutic. I believe this to be violence. This has caused many to question the relevance of the church and faith in God. These are church hurts and they have caused many to walk away.

I was once a member of a church in the Washington, DC area. The church was living, vibrant, and filled with many opportunities that facilitated spiritual growth. However, I encountered many lay leaders who were pious, condemnatory, and controlling. They spent time in cliques that were riddled with gossip. It felt like they squeezed every ounce of joy out of our souls by constantly berating us with their rules. I love music and dancing. Once I mentioned that I was attending a listening party for a new artist at a venue on U Street. These women looked at me as if I said I was going to conduct a round of drive-by shootings. "You shouldn't do that," remarked one. "You need a mentor," stated the other. These types of comments were made often as they would look down their noses at those whom they perceived to be less than spiritually mature.

This line of behavior also caused them to fight for control. They withheld positions and leadership roles for those within the clique only– those who met their spiritual expectations. I found dealing with these lay leaders isolating, hurtful, and draining.

Dealing with situations such as this makes leaving the church and in some instances, God, a reasonable solution. What I had to realize was that identifying a church is like making any other long-term commitment, such as buying a home, identifying a life partner, etc. It's not one size fits all but we keep shopping until we find the match. It doesn't mean we give up. I have also realized that we may outgrow a space or our spiritual needs change. It's ok.

Dealing with lay leaders who are not emotionally whole can bring us damage. This also leaves us with lots of questions. Many stray away because we were conditioned not to ask those hard questions.

As a child, I heard the elders say, "You should never question God." I'm sure we all have heard this before, right? This notion of questioning God as blasphemy was passed down from slave owners who wanted to keep the enslaved docile. This idea spread to those outside of slave plantations. However, this left us with even more questions and less understanding. I've noticed that as new generations arise they desire answers to the questions we were afraid to ask.

As church leaders, Shamon and I realize that people attend church for one of four reasons- to gain answers, to obtain community, out of tradition, or to find purpose. We have noticed that when people begin to turn away from God they start by removing themselves from church. Next, they ask the hard questions:

If an omniscient, omnipotent God exists, why does He allow people to face food insecurities?

If God exists why didn't he strike down those that abused and misused their power?

Why does He allow terrible things to happen to innocent children?

Why did God allow slavery and genocide?
and the list goes on and on

When people do not have answers to these questions, they turn to a place that can provide an answer they can digest. Sometimes that means it's easier to believe that there is no God than to accept that horrible things happened on His watch.

Not being able to question God makes Him seem distant. It's easier to walk away from something that doesn't appear to be accessible to you. These are some of the reasons we are seeing an overall decline in church participation and Christianity. Food for thought: In the past twenty-five years, forty million Americans have stopped attending church.[1] Some walk away from the belief in God all altogether. Others turn to worship the creation itself and ancestral worship. In any case, people go where they believe answers lie and to what may feel more comfortable to them.

Contrary to what we have been taught, God is very open to us asking hard questions. These conversations allow us to become intimate with Him. Let me explain; when my kids ask me questions, it allows us to engage and interact. This becomes a very intimate time for us because we are getting to see what we believe and how we think. So it is with God. We can understand the mind of God and build a relationship with Him when we inquire. He's not embarrassed or angry with us when we ask hard questions –in fact He welcomes it.

I began asking the hard questions in 1995. It was during this time that my grandmother became ill. She, like many other Black Americans from her generation, did not trust the medical community. So she never sought answers for the illness she felt. One night, while she was sound asleep she dreamed that her deceased father, whom she loved dearly, said to her, "Sister please go see a doctor." Her visit to the doctor was where she discovered she had colon cancer. After performing more tests, they discovered it was severe and the cancer had spread to other vital organs. The doctors ordered her to have immediate surgery followed by a round of chemo and radiation. This particular combination would prolong her life for another year and a half, at best giving her more time to prepare her affairs.

My grandmother was what the old folks referred to as a prayer warrior. She prayed all day and night. Not only did she pray all hours of the day, but it was how she prayed that made the difference– loud and hard. She prayed without ceasing. Because of her tireless devotion, I used to think of her as Jesus' little sister. This made it difficult for me to understand why a loving God would allow this to happen to a person who had devoted her life to Him.

As my grandmother continued to pray and held fast to her faith, she told us that Jesus wanted her to refuse the chemo and radiation. As her family, we were shocked. We were believers in modern medicine and trusted the doctor's advice so this brought us angst. Even after many conversations with my grandmother, we knew ultimately, the decision was out of our hands.

Refusing the chemo and radiation, my grandmother decided to treat herself. She made drastic lifestyle changes—improving her diet by eating whole clean foods (before healthy eating was a trend). She increased her intake of herbs and began to exercise. Surpassing the doctor's expectations my grandmother did not pass away until June of 2006, almost ten and a half years later. Even her doctors considered her a miracle.

Three things are certain to occur in life– suffering, loss, and uncertainty. Regardless of who we choose not to worship, those things will always exist. God gave us Jesus and not only is He the one who atones for us but He gives all that we need to survive and make sense of challenging times.

The truth is Jesus called us to become disciples and to follow Him and the words He spoke. As a result, God's divinely inspired words have certainly been misunderstood, misinterpreted, and misconstrued as a tool to abuse many–that we must acknowledge.

While on earth, Jesus loved people; He loved everybody. He loved the oppressed, the broken-hearted, the disabled, the whores, the harlots, the poor, the mourners, and even those who played a major part in His murder– Judas. Only a loving superhuman would think, "I know you will betray me and have me killed but instead of hating you I will spend time with you and put you in charge of my finances." This also shows us the power of knowing our identity and purpose. When we know who we are and why we are here, we don't give our energy to hating anyone and no one makes us feel threatened.

What He requires of us is love. He wants us to love and build a relationship with Him. From that relationship, He would like for us to live in community with each other which is why the Bible says, "It's not good for man to be alone."[1] Out of that community, we should continue His works of supporting each other, rebuking oppression, healing, and bringing hope to those who are hurting. That collective community can be the church.

One of the most influential institutions we have in our community is the Black church. It is the place where slave ancestors held meetings to discuss plans to revolt or escape to freedom. It served as the very foundation on which the Civil Rights movement rested. Faith in God gave our ancestors the courage to gain freedom:

PBS states, "Nothing was more graphic for the slaves than the story of the children of Israel being led out of bondage."[3] Faith in Jesus as well as the scriptures in the Bible gave our ancestors the courage to seek freedom.

Abolitionist Nat Turner led the bloodiest slave revolt in US history using the scriptures in the Bible as his reason. When he was captured, in hand was his Bible.[4]

Ebenezer Baptist Church in Atlanta was founded by former slaves. Under the leadership of Dr. Martin Luther King Jr, this church hosted many civil rights meetings and discussions.[5]

St. Augustine's Episcopal Church in West Oakland CA was the location in which the Black

Panther's Free Breakfast program was launched. This program provided meals to Black children in impoverished urban neighborhoods. By the end of 1969, this program had fed over 20,000 children.[6]

Rev. Francis Griffin of First Baptist Church in Farmville is known as the "fighting preacher" because he believed that, "All forms of worship should be related to a form of action." Throughout the 1950s, he led the fight for education as he pushed to provide alternate forms of education for Black children who didn't have access to the public school system.[7]

More recently, it was the place where almost every R&B and gospel singer and musician (Whitney Houston, John Legend, Toni Braxton, Usher, Monica, Justin Timberlake, Jagged Edge) discovered they had a God-given gift. That gift launched them into very successful careers.

The Black church is just as much a part of our culture as Dr. Martin Luther King Jr, The Cosby Show, HBCUs, Beyonce, spades tournaments, summer cook-outs, collard greens, macaroni and cheese, line dancing, and "Before I Let Go" by Frankie Beverly.

Faith in the Saviour, the one who changed the game millions of years ago along with the Bible isn't about shame and ridicule, it's about hope, love, courage, and redemption. It's about abolishing systems that are harmful and in stark contrast to our flawed human experience. It is about believing in those far-fetched stories in the Bible because true faith requires us to stretch beyond our tangible realm to believe in something larger than our limited thinking.

We leave you with this:

"Everything is possible for one who believes."
— **Mark 9:23**

Questions for Reflection:

1. How was God viewed in your family during your childhood?

2. How often was church attendance in your family during childhood?

3. How do you view faith today?

4. What situations have challenged and tested your faith?

5. What were some positive experiences you have had at church?

6. What were some negative experiences you had at church?

7. Did you see a therapist after the negative experiences at church? If you didn't, how do you believe that would have helped you?

8. List three people who you know have strong faith.

Activity

Spend time in silence for about 5-10 minutes each day asking God to speak to you. Write down what you hear and feel during that time.

Chapter 11

The Wounds of Time

"The key is in not spending time, but in investing it."
– **Stephen R. Covey**

Nijiama

As a child, everyone in my family worked hard and long hours. Therefore, my family was never the type to engage in impromptu trips to the park, do arts and crafts on a Saturday afternoon, or fly kites on a windy day. As a kid, I felt like I was always surrounded by adults and forced to listen to adult conversations so I spent most of my time daydreaming. I spent hours in my head envisioning a life that was far different from my own. I assume that was my way of dissociating.

I believe that freedom is something that every kid dreams of and at that time I wanted nothing more than to be free. So most of my daydreaming involved being a teenager with a driver's license and car. Then as a teenager, my daydreaming switched to being a college student living in the dorms while participating in all of the college happenings. Once in college, I began dreaming about being educated, young, and single while living in a big city. This is where my relationship with time began.

I spent many years anticipating the next moment or the next phase in life while never truly enjoying the present. Once the moment passed, I regretted my lack of presence.

Anticipating the future also meant that I was putting happiness off for my future self to enjoy instead of digesting the happiness that was in front of me. So as an adult, I have to teach myself to live in the moment. This is a constant reminder for me. I had to heal the wound because I felt that I had lost time by not being present and that was bringing me angst.

Many of us are mourning because we have lost time whether we spent it being incarcerated, dealing with addiction, or at the mercy of mental health issues. I also know many individuals who felt they lost time, particularly their younger years because it was spent invested in failed relationships. They believed they should have used that time to pursue education, and careers, or simply enjoy being carefree. To prevent these regrets from turning into bitterness, we have to learn to forgive ourselves. We have to extend grace to ourselves understanding that we made the decisions that reflected where we were at the time.

We have to be mindful of how we spend our present and future, even when we are in situations where our time is constrained such as imprisonment. We can still use that time productively. Curtis Carroll spent those years of imprisonment studying and improving himself. He has stated that he read over 500 financial articles per week while serving his sentence. Today, he uses that knowledge to improve the lives of many. He made a horrible decision many years ago, served his time, and transformed into living a life of service to mankind. In addition to paying his debt for his actions, his prison sentence was God's means of redirecting the course of his life. When we understand that even during our darkest times, God can still use us to be a blessing to others we become transformed. He is the truest redeemer of time. That perspective is how we regain our power.

Time is something to be honored. Many people sell their time to organizations in exchange for money every single day– employment. That portrays the value of time. Therefore, let's honor time and eliminate time wasters.

We also need to honor the time of others. If we know we have no plans to marry the person we are dating and they want that, let's not waste their time. If we know we can't be faithful, let's not waste that person's time, emotions, and resources by marrying them. If we know we are not going to give the time stated in the job description or contract, let's not accept the position or opportunity.

Although we can't go back to the past we can indeed reclaim our time by focusing on the present and how we can give our whole self to the moment we are in.

Shamon

The Philadelphia 76ers, an NBA basketball team, has a "tagline" that speaks to the term the value of time and that motto is "Trust the Process". Let me break it down for you. In some cases, a team forgoes the opportunity to "win now" by putting themselves in position by any means possible versus setting themselves up for sustained long-term success. As the 76ers were looking to build long-term success, what they let go of were declining players and exorbitant contracts, which they considered liabilities for younger players, some with questionable health and potential.

This approach from the outside made the 76ers look foolish because the news was that they were sending away assets to help the win-now teams and taking on a bunch of liabilities. However, leaders across the organization and even in their marketing campaigns kept uttering to those who were invested to "Trust the Process".

What we all find out as we study value and time is that a liability isn't truly a liability, it just needs time to be nurtured and matured. Over time those "liabilities" became the most tremendous assets and the time it took to achieve the promise paid for itself and then some. My marriage, my children, and more importantly, who am I now had to go through that nurturing and maturing process to yield the immense results that I now enjoy in life today. The storms of arguments, absence of loved ones, infertility issues, financial setbacks, and being rejected for countless opportunities in the workspace and in the church had sharpened me to be the best version of myself. We all have a way of thinking or acting now that appears to be an asset, but in the places, we're trying to go in the future, it's going to require a "rebuilding process". The thing is this: your success will be stifled or capped if you aren't willing to rebuild – and to do that, it's going to take investing in the most invaluable commodity known to mankind to accomplish, which is time.

Questions for Reflection

1. In what significant ways do you believe you wasted time in the past? Have you forgiven yourself?

2. What do you believe are time wasters in your life today?

3. How can you be more present in each moment?

Chapter 12

Healing

"The healing process is ugly as hell. It's not bubble baths and aromatherapy. It's accountability which brings guilt. It's getting to the root of your issues which is triggering and painful. Processing trauma often means you have to relive it which isn't easy but it's worth it."
Author unknown

Nijiama

Placing spaghetti inside of Tupperware is always a bad idea. It's difficult to remove the red pasta stains from Tupperware if it sits too long. Although the dish may be filled with broccoli and cheese, the Tupperware container may still appear to be filled with spaghetti from the outside. So it is with us if we do not heal. Our joy will be overshadowed by the effects of our unhealed wounds. Our light will be dimmed by the pain and our wounds will continue to wreak havoc in our lives. I believe most humans have a desire to be whole and to have their relationships and decisions reflect the wholeness that is inside of them. For this reason, healing has become a very popular term. But people become stuck with what is true healing and where to begin.

What is even more problematic is the way our society handles mental and emotional health. Our brain is the most powerful organ in our body. It generates enough electricity to power a lightbulb. It controls breathing, vision, hunger, movement and so much more. Yet we do not care for it as much as we care for other essential organs. To date, we have a reactive approach to mental and emotional health. It is only when we are in a crisis that we seek therapeutic services. We would be much better off if we developed a proactive approach. Just as we regularly ensure that our kidneys, liver, and heart operate at optimal levels, we should provide the same care for our brain. And that is how we framed this discussion on healing. We are not only providing tools to overcome our past and present emotional trauma but resources to monitor our health and a plan for overall long-term mental health care. The world we live in can be such an ugly place with heartbreak being inevitable. We all need techniques that are real and actionable that can be implemented almost immediately whether we are in an emotional health crisis or not.

Self-Awareness —Know Thyself

Nijiama

I have a friend who complains that it is hard to make friends in our forties. She recalls when we were in our early twenties and women appeared more open to making new friends and people were much easier to get along with. Similarly to Charlotte, once she makes a new friend and they do or say something that rubs her the wrong way, she internalizes it, makes it about her, and replays it over and over in her mind. This process makes her bitter towards them and eventually, she acts on the bitterness. She begins excluding them from social events, gossiping about them, and distancing herself from them. Like a ball of snow, all of this slowly mounts into friction between her and the friend and before you know it the two have completely fallen out.

This becomes my friend's pattern with almost everyone she encounters and every time, she blames them. She has yet to look inwardly to see her part in the downfall of the relationships.

Many of us behave in this manner, to some degree. We only see the parts of ourselves that we want to see while ignoring what we either can't handle or refuse to see. This leads us to more inner confusion. A less-than-self-aware person often comes across as deeply immature because self-awareness leads to growth. It requires time to one's self to introspect and the ability to withstand the pain of acknowledging our flaws to become self-aware.

The first step in this process of healing is understanding that there is a gap between how we are showing up today and how we want and need to show up to live a pleasing life. My friend, for example, desires friendships but she has to look at how she handles conflict. Jared and Charlotte have not realized that the way they are showing up impacts their loved ones and the people around them.

If we want to own a successful business, we will need to learn how to work with the most difficult of people. If we want to become a leader we will need to develop emotional intelligence. If we want to enjoy a life surrounded by love we will need to understand how to extend grace and forgiveness. All of this requires solid emotional health and emotional intelligence.

We want to point out that self-awareness is not easy. It requires us to take a step back and admit to ourselves, "I may have been wrong in XYZ situation." It also requires us to acknowledge that some of the core beliefs that we inherited from our caregivers may be causing us more harm than good.

The means to understanding who we are and how we are showing up is to be open and honest with ourselves and consider what has triggered us lately or what has caused us to feel anger or hurt.

Trigger Mapping Exercise

Nijiama

If we want to understand where our wounds lie we can begin by paying attention to how we behave when we are triggered. Defined by the "Cambridge Dictionary" triggered means
to experience a strong emotional reaction of fear, shock, anger, or worry, especially because you are made to remember something bad that
has happened in the past.[1]

Triggers will lead us to our wounds. In the example in the introduction, Charlotte was triggered by being overwhelmed with critical information. During the school meeting, the information left her feeling helpless. In response to the discomfort, she lashed out. That was her way of trying to scramble for control of the situation. It was also her immature way of saying, *this conversation was hard and uncomfortable for me.*
In the chart on the next page, describe the most recent or most profound situation in which you experienced the feeling or trigger. Jot your answers to each of the sections associated with the feeling. Be open and honest as you consider what has triggered you lately and how it has caused you to react.

Trigger (The emotion)	Describe the Situation	My Reaction -How did I handle it?	Was my reaction helpful or harmful?	What were the feelings I experienced about the event?	Memory of experiencing in childhood or adolescence.
Overlooked					
Disrespected					
Lied to					
Belittled					
Denied					
Rejected					
Left out					
Unloved					
Betrayed					
Unseen / Unheard					
Judged					
Blamed					

Belief Systems

Nijiama

Behind each trigger, there is a belief about ourselves that we may have embraced during the darkest times. These beliefs shape how we move throughout the world. For example, The lack of affirmation Jared received as a child from his father causes him to believe he is not good enough. So he puts forth quite a bit of effort proving to the world that he is good enough so that he can gain applause from others—the approval that his father couldn't provide.

Quinten has placed a high priority on being a ladies' man. He believes this to be important as it is the one area in which he sees himself as a winner. So he looks and dresses the part to attract as many women as he possibly can gain. He also enjoys the attention of women as it is the validation he never received as a child.

Charlotte has many hurts that roam inside of her. Through lashing out, yelling, and making threats, she believes she gains her power back from past situations that left her feeling powerless.

Sabrina sees herself as a victim. She believes God has abandoned her and faith didn't work as it should so she moves from one paradigm to the next trying to find identity and safety.

It is so important that we love ourselves, validate our experiences and exercise self-compassion. This looks like saying to ourselves, "You had a rough childhood and made some decisions based on that but you survived, and it's ok."

As we eradicate the beliefs that no longer serve us, we need to do things to soothe ourselves. These activities will be especially helpful for us during times when we are feeling low; watching a funny movie or video, praying, talking with a close friend, or seeing a therapist. These are all activities that can nourish our souls.

Questions for Reflection

1. How did you soothe yourself as a child?

2. How do you soothe yourself today? Is it healthy?

Acceptance

Nijiama

While I was speaking during a women's retreat, one of the women attending, Linda, mentioned that her mother favored her biracial older sister over her. With tears in her eyes, she pointed out to me example after example and instance after instance of her mother favoring her sister over her. Her sister attended private school and she didn't. Her sister was taken on shopping trips and vacations while she was left to remain at home. Her mother often doted on her sister and maintained a close relationship with her. As Linda kept talking, I noticed that she questioned why her mother had treated her differently and why her mother wouldn't admit it. Linda believed it was unfair, and that her mother needed to own it, explain it, and make attempts to make it right. I realized then Linda had not accepted it.

We have to come to terms with the fact that life isn't fair and the people in our lives will not always do what's right by us. We can't change people. We can only change ourselves and our reactions and that is where the true power lies. To have inner peace, we have to make peace with the disgusting parts of life. When we wrestle with it, as Linda did, constantly questioning it and thirsting for answers we may never receive, the pain is kept alive inside of us. And that pain will impact almost every single area of our lives.

Often when we are triggered it is an indicator that we have yet to make peace with our past hurts. Of those hurts, in our minds, we think;

- *It's not supposed to be this way.*
- *My mother was not supposed to be addicted to drugs and abandon me.*
- *Why did I have to be born to an abusive father?*
- *I shouldn't have gotten pregnant at seventeen years old.*
- *Why did I have a parent suffering from mental illness?*

Those thoughts behave like rain watering plants, or in this case, our wounds, causing them to grow larger and larger.

Getting to acceptance isn't easy– it's a process. We must start the process by mourning that which we have lost or didn't receive. In the example of Linda, she must mourn the relationship she would have liked to have had with her mother or the way she believes her mother should have behaved towards her. She must allow the emotions to flow and lean into them while letting go of her ideals of what her relationship with her mom should have looked like. Linda has to learn to live in the reality of the situation– acknowledging the fact that her mother treats her differently.

After mourning, moving towards acceptance means seeing the good that she may have gained from this situation. As I continued to listen to Linda, I noticed that she was really in the best position in this situation. Because of her mother's close relationship with her sister, her mother was very critical of her sister's behavior and actions. Her mother was living through her sister and that was causing her to control her sister's every move. Linda, on the other hand, was free from that behavior. She was free to be who she wanted to be and do whatever she wanted to do without criticism. Acceptance allows us to see and appreciate the good in even the darkest of situations. It forced Linda to take her eyes off of her sister and what she believed her sister had and placed her eyes on herself to see all that she had gained; strength, resilience, independence, and freedom.

It's so important that we understand that there are often gifts we gain from trauma. The things that are the problems in our lives can and will become the gifts in our lives if we can just withstand the discomfort.

Once you achieve acceptance you will be able to stare at the pain that once held you captive and be completely indifferent to it and that alone is emotional freedom. Acceptance looks like having the ability to acknowledge the offense but without pain, without frustration, and judgment. You may even begin to laugh when you think of it because soon joy will fill the place where pain once lived. Acceptance is understanding that the situation is not what you wanted but you learned to live with it.

As a whole, Black America can benefit from embracing acceptance. Not only do we wrestle with the pain of our enslaved ancestors but the aftermath that we dealt with as well; the racist laws, ordinances, and devices that plagued us from Reconstruction to the Civil Rights era such as Jim Crow, Klan attacks, and police brutality. And being treated like second-class citizens in what was deemed "the land of the free."

Racism affects us and serves as our trigger. Because of that, when we see white supremacists march through the town of Charlottesville, VA, or when we are referred to as the n-word we are triggered. As Black Americans, we must accept that there will always be racists and racism. The US was built on slave labor fueled by racism so it will likely never die. We must get to a place in which we can stare a racist in the eye and be unmoved going on about our day. We fight not with our hands but with legislation, knowledge, mobilization, and power that we create. Acceptance is powerful and it makes forgiveness easier.

Questions for Reflection

1. What are some situations you need to accept? For each situation you listed, consider if there is anything good that you have gained from the experience.

2. List ten gifts you have gained from the trauma you experienced.

Forgiveness

Nijiama

Now we know you say to yourself, "Every time I pick up one of these self-help books it talks about forgiveness." True. Shamon and I want you to understand that a crucial part of healing is forgiveness. However, there are so many myths regarding forgiveness which makes it a struggle to understand what forgiveness is and isn't.

Forgiveness doesn't mean we must apologize or vocalize to our offender that we have forgiven them. It doesn't mean our offender or violator should not face consequences for their actions. Forgiveness doesn't mean we must hug them, spend time with them, talk to them, or allow them to have access to us. What forgiveness does mean, in simple terms, is that from every single fiber of our being, we have let it go. Just as we exhale air from our lungs, we exhale the pain their action inflicted upon us. We remove them from living inside of our emotions. We will know when we have let it go when we can see them or hear their name called and not feel any negative emotions towards them. We no longer spend time talking about what they did in a way that is negative or mentally ponder over the pain they have caused; neither do we patiently wait for justice to be served on them. We simply let it be.

Now let me say forgiveness is not easy. Some of us have been deeply hurt in the past or are even in harmful situations as of this minute. What helps us forgive is understanding the offender's backstory. For those of us who may have been harmed by our parents, this is the reason why understanding transgenerational trauma is so powerful. It helps us to empathize and understand the circumstances surrounding their behavior. Again, the point is not to excuse their wrong but for us to no longer be held captive by the pain.

A year ago, when my mother came for a visit, I was able to wrap my arms around her, look her in the eye, and say to her, "I'm sorry you did not receive the love and care you needed as a child." I now am capable of understanding that she has a backstory that impacted how she parented. By forgiving, her pain is no longer mine to carry. Her trauma is no longer in my hands to pass on to the future.

Regardless of what we have been told or believe, holding on to the offense causes us harm. It doesn't eradicate the wrong they have done to us and it certainly doesn't unleash a hail of wrath upon them. What it does, however, is hold us captive. Dr. Bessel Van Der Kolk shows us in *The Body Keeps the Score* that when we haven't forgiven, we may treat our loved ones who offend us even in the mildest sense the way we wish we had treated those who harmed us.[2] Our loved ones do not deserve that.

The way to achieve forgiveness is to decide to let it go. It's an active decision because you have to make the choice and not simply just hope it will go away. Decide it's not your battle to fight or your grudge to hold. Give it to God, literally. Every time a negative thought about that person comes to your mind, say the following out loud:

I Choose To Let It Go. I Choose Forgiveness. I Choose My Peace.

Quickly eliminate the negative thoughts from your mind. Don't entertain it; not even for a second because it will take you back to a place of pain.

The consequence of unforgiveness is bitterness. In a nutshell, bitterness is unforgiveness that lingers and turns to anger. Many walk among us today with hearts filled with bitterness. Living with bitterness is similar to living with poison in our bodies– it will make us emotionally sick. It changes the way we see things, causing us to see only the negative and constantly complain. It causes us to take the slightest things personally. It also makes us difficult to live with and relationships a challenge. Bitterness will place us in a perpetual state of self-sabotage.

Questions for Reflection

1. Who do you need to forgive? What is preventing you from forgiving them?

2. Who do you owe an apology? What is preventing you from apologizing?

Activity

For the person to whom you owe an apology, if you have access to them and you believe it will remain peaceful, reach out to them and extend the apology. Journal your thoughts on this. Discuss this with your therapist, if you have one, asking them to guide you through this exercise.

Change your Perspective

Nijiama

When I was a wedding planner, one of the first pieces of advice I would share with my brides was that on the day of, something would go wrong. You see most brides have been sold the myth of a perfect wedding day. So, when the cake arrives ten minutes late, the caterer runs out of beer, or grandma gets lost on her way to the reception, the bride has an epic meltdown because she believes the incident ruined her perfect day. I reminded them that every single person in their wedding including the vendors are flawed humans. Therefore, something will go wrong– it's inevitable. There are also many factors outside of our control such as the weather and natural disasters that can impact the day. This level sets the expectations and when things go wrong, they can move past it because they are prepared for it.

One of the most profound changes to my perspective has been accepting the fact that people are human and bound to disappoint us. No one is perfect nor idealistic; our parents are not the characters on television, our fathers are not superheroes, and our friends aren't without flaws. They are human beings before they wear any of those titles. Because of their humanity, they are bound to make mistakes which often leads to our disappointments. Most of our discouragement comes from allowing human flawed behavior to overwhelm us, make us angry, and lead us to unforgiveness.

I used to watch old episodes of *Leave It To Beaver* when I was much younger. I saw a picture-perfect family who lived in a white picket-fenced home in the suburbs. The mother, June Cleaver, was an agreeable, stay-at-home mom who assured them a hot meal was on the table waiting for them to arrive from work and school. The father, Ward Cleaver, brought home the bacon and was there every night to help the Beaver and his brother Wally work through life lessons.[3] I knew that this show did not represent my family however as a kid I longed for some of this. This is what I thought was normal. The truth is this show didn't represent most American families. Quite like the four families mentioned in the introduction, life for many of us may be vastly different from the picture-perfect ideals we have embraced or what we believe is normal. It may appear unfair and feel as if we have been forsaken. We have to remind ourselves that regardless of what our past looked like or the circumstances we were born into, we can still have a good life today. Life is messy and everyone's normal may differ.

Questions for Reflection

1. How have you handled your most recent disappointments?

2. How does conflict make you feel?

3. How do you handle criticism/ feedback from others?

Vulnerability

Nijiama

In Sept. 2023, Grammy award-winning gospel artist Kirk Franklin released his documentary *Father's Day* which shows Mr. Franklin's mother denying the results of a paternity test. The test proved that the man he believed to be his father wasn't. He learned that a different man, Richard Hubbard, was his father. What I, like many others, found to be even more jarring was that although the men took the test twice producing the same results, his mother continued to claim the results were false. It was tough to watch.

This can sometimes be the behavior of our elders. My grandmother shared similar sentiments as she would say to us, "Don't tell the family's business." There was a lot of fear in this type of statement. This generation lived during a time when people believed that secrets were protection. They didn't value living in truth or authenticity as many do now particularly if they felt their truth would bring them shame and judgment. So, they hid the parts of them that they just couldn't deal with. However, family secrets often hurt and damage the ones we love the most.

What we keep secret, we have not made peace with nor healed from. Keeping secrets is harmful to our emotional health. Shame dwells in our secrets and chips away at our self-esteem. The Bible, on the other hand, tells us that "the truth shall set us free."[7] When we share, we are healing. We are also processing verbally which is why talk therapy is so popular. You can't break the cycle if it's hidden and swept under the rug. That which we cannot share still keeps us bound. And that which we are bound by, we become emotionally sensitive too. This is how secrets damage families. It will become a haunting trigger for us. When we share, the sting of shame and guilt is gone and that is emotional freedom. We also remove the power from others because now that we have exposed it, no one can use it against us.

There is another side of vulnerability and that is articulating when we are offended. You see, this was hard for me because my family didn't verbalize offenses, at least not in a healthy way. We saw conflict as a bad thing. When someone hurt or offended us, we distanced ourselves from them and told everyone else about the offense hoping they'd relay the information. A few years later, we resume the relationship until something happens that reminds us of the pain, causing us to explode.

Vulnerability is powerful because it requires us to look a person in the eyes and say, "You have hurt me and I need to understand why" or, as Auntie Oprah Winfrey encourages us to ask, "What happened to us?"[5] This requires courage, confidence, and emotional regulation. After all, having these conversations means we have to sit in an uncomfortable moment. It may also cause us to become triggered and hypervigilance will rear its ugly head. Regardless of the feelings that arise, it is the safest way to move through relationships.

It also creates safety so that people feel comfortable sharing when we hurt them. We need to truly listen with our whole heart when our loved ones share with us their hurts particularly if we are the ones that caused it. I had to learn to listen–without judgment, without my defenses up, and without excuses. I believe there is some level of truth to everyone's story and we need to be willing to accept it. We shouldn't want any of our loved ones to feel victimized by us so we should ask, "How can I give you the best of me?" If they genuinely love us, they will give us answers that don't include having to compromise ourselves.

Vulnerability is also counter-cultural because many of us believe that we need to confront and when doing so we must be tough, guarded, and defensive. On the other hand, vulnerability requires us to swallow our pride and embrace humility. In these moments, we are seeking to understand instead of forcing ourselves to be understood.

To all of my friends, I say to them, "I'm a flawed human and will disappoint you but that's not my aim. Please let me be the first to know when I have disappointed you." I want us to hash it out with vulnerability and love instead of repeating bad behavior which will ultimately destroy the relationship.

Questions for Reflection

1. List secrets that plague your family. How have they impacted the family? What would change if the secrets were out? What would be some good things that can come from the secrets being revealed?

2. Describe a situation in which you saw someone display vulnerability.

3. How has your lack of vulnerability impacted your life?

4. What do you fear, if anything, about being vulnerable?

Activity
Ask the top 5 people who are the closest to you how you can give them the best of you.

The Technique—Self-Regulation

Nijiama

A few years ago, I hosted an event at my home. I invited some of my colleagues, church members, and a few neighbors to the event. It was catered by a local chef who served a delicious menu and tasty beverages. We spent the evening networking, mixing, mingling, and laughing. One of my neighbors, who was in attendance, was a married young woman who graduated from Harvard Law School. She is an attorney who has a very successful career.

As the spirits began flowing and the conversation became more about serious topics, she grew upset with me because we didn't share the same belief on a hot-button issue. I could see that she was rather passionate about the issue and my stance made her uncomfortable. So, I encouraged everyone to change the conversation to keep the moment light. Out of her frustrations, she referred to me as a four-letter derogatory name so I told her if she wasn't able to calm down she would need to leave.

To make a very long story short, she grew increasingly upset and threatened to attack me–in my home. She yelled from the top of her lungs, "I'm going to f#$% you up!" It took three women to remove her from my home as she yelled and cursed. Out of concern for her driving home, while intoxicated, we called her husband to pick her up. When he arrived, she still refused to leave as she stood on my front lawn in our upper-middle-class suburban neighborhood in the early hours of the morning threatening to attack me.

The next day, when we played the footage from that night from my security cameras, we heard her yelling,

"My house is three times bigger than this one!"

"My Mercedes is better than her car!"

Immediately, when I heard that my anger towards this sister (yes, I was pissed, don't get it twisted) turned to sadness for her. Her comments and reactions were a trauma response. Somehow, she was triggered and reacted poorly because she didn't have the tools to regulate herself. On that night, her pride had gotten the better of her, quite the way Jared's pride gets the better of him. Pride is so fragile as it often serves as the buffer for low self-worth. She grew upset because she felt her self-worth was upended. At that moment, instead of wanting to choke her out, I wanted to wrap my arms around her and let her know that she is valued with or without her title, with or without her degrees, and with or without her cars.

The lesson in this for all of us is that at any time we can be triggered. It's up to us as mature, well-adjusted, professional, adults to know how to manage our triggers so that we can avoid damaging our relationships or ruining our credibility. Acting on impulses is a very primitive response that we often see emulated by lower beings such as animals. As more advanced beings, we need to master self-regulation which requires us to gain control of our emotions and tap into the rational side of our brain.

This doesn't simply apply to situations in which we want to throw hands, this also can be applied to any situation in which we could make a decision that could damage or drastically change our lives for the worse. One of the biggest questions we need to ask ourselves is– how do we prevent the worst of us from showing up?

The self-regulation technique can be broken down into three easy steps called the three R's:

1. Remain Calm
2. Reframe Negative Thoughts
3. Recall the Consequences

Remain Calm

It is so important that we remain calm during intense situations. The reason is because when we become angry or flustered, our heart rate and testosterone production increase, cortisol (the stress hormone) decreases, and the left part of the brain, which controls our emotions, becomes highly stimulated. Immediately, the fight, flight, or freeze response becomes ignited.[6] Our thoughts become irrational making it difficult for wise decision-making to occur. When we are in this state, we rely on our most primitive instincts. We give in to what our impulse tells us to do whether it's fighting, threatening violence, overeating, or having reckless sex. This is what happens to Charlotte. She becomes overstimulated, angry, and irrational.

Remaining calm, on the other hand, helps us to think clearly instead of allowing our feelings and unregulated nervous system to control us. It prevents us from doing things that are potentially harmful to us or others.

I was at my son's baseball game when two parents got into a heated argument. One of the parents attacked the other parent with a metal water bottle. As a result, in front of the children, coaches, and his own family, he was placed in handcuffs and taken to jail. If he had the ability to remain calm, he would have been able to make a more rational decision instead of one that places his future in jeopardy.

To remain calm during intense situations, we must take two to three deep breaths. Then take a mindful moment. At that moment, take notice of everything around us; note what we smell, what we see, and can touch. This will calm emotions, reduce hypervigilance, and allow rational thinking to prevail.

Reframe Our Thoughts

The thoughts we have about a person or situation is often the place that leads us to inner chaos. We have to control our thoughts and check our perceptions because they may be incorrect, unnecessary, or harmful. For each of the scenarios mentioned in the introduction, there are thoughts that led to bad behavior.

For Charlotte, she allowed her mind to develop negative thoughts regarding the school meeting. Charlotte had embraced the stigma surrounding special education services for children. Had she reframed it to believe that the school administrators had a desire to see her child gain the tools he needs to be successful, the conversation would have gone much more smoothly.

There may be times when we can't seem to gain control of our negative thoughts. We may find these thoughts are constant and overwhelming. There may also be times where it may feel as if the negative thoughts grow and take on their own form building upon each other, developing their own narratives. These false narratives are harmful and control our moods and actions towards others. This can be linked to anxiety and other mental health issues. In these instances, we need to seek help from a professional such as a psychotherapist as soon as possible.

Recall the Consequences

The final step in self-regulation is recalling the consequences. Regardless of the situation we are in, there will always be a space between our trigger and our reaction. We need to take advantage of that space and use it to consider the consequences. In this moment, we need to ask ourselves the following:

What will be the consequences if I do XYZ?

Can I live with the consequences?

Is this going to be helpful or harmful to me in the long run?

There are many people today who live with regret. Quite like Quentin, there are people who regret having unprotected sex. Many people regret pulling the trigger on a firearm. I'm sure some regret stealing the car. Eliminating a lifetime of regrets begins with self-regulation.

Questions for Reflection

1. Consider several moments in the past in which you believe using the 3 R method could have been beneficial for you. How would things be different for you?

Self-Care

Nijiama

Self-care is a big trendy word that recently became popular. Albeit trendy, it is necessary. Self-care is the preventive part of emotional health because it focuses on brain care while healing hypervigilance.

Many of us grew up partially raised by a Big Momma. A member of the silent generation, Big Momma was indeed an alpha mom who dealt with more than her fair share of racism, poverty, and oppression. She was tough and gritty but had a big heart.

By the time Big Momma was forty years old, she was overweight and constantly complaining of exhaustion as she wore moo-moo dresses. "There is just so much on me," she often lamented. Before she even reached her fifties, Big Momma was suffering from hypertension, diabetes, and achy knees. Why? because Big Momma placed everyone else's needs before her own. Her days became filled with cooking huge meals so everyone would have a full belly even those in the community. She babysat her grandchildren and was at the beck and call of her adult children, bailing them out of the harmful situations they were in even at her own financial and emotional expense. This type of behavior has become a part of our culture.

There was no time for our elders to practice self-care because they had to work, pay bills, and take care of everybody. Because of this, their health suffered.

Self-care is soul care. We can't engage in soul care without implementing strong boundaries. Boundaries are protection– they protect our souls, emotions, and relationships, and help us to maintain inner peace. Boundaries begin with the word No.

For Big Momma, her boundaries should have looked like this:

- No, I'm not using my pension to save my adult child from mistakes they willingly made.
- No, I'm not going to take out a second mortgage on my house to keep my son out of jail for his drug charges.
- No, my adult children and grandchildren can't live in my home indefinitely and not help pay bills nor participate in the maintenance of the house.
- No, I don't have to babysit my grandchildren and great-grandchildren if I'm not feeling up to it or have other plans.
- No, my husband can't have me and a second family on the side too.

Examples of boundaries we can implement look like:

- ✓ No, you can't curse me out and disrespect me or my loved ones
- ✓ No, I can't listen to R. Kelly's music because it will cause me to chase sex
- ✓ No, I'm not going to gossip with my friend about my other friends

- ✓ No, I will not get drunk because I can't control myself
- ✓ No, I will not bond with you over a common enemy
- ✓ No, you can't ride with me to the event if you are going to be 40 minutes late
- ✓ No, I'm not going to do anything that goes against my values or makes me feel uncomfortable to maintain a relationship
- ✓ No, I will never convince a woman to do anything that strips them of their dignity or they are not 100% comfortable with

Please remember that boundaries must have consequences.

As we move through our healing process, we may realize that the behavior of our loved ones may be emotionally immature, or even toxic. Especially if we have suffered from betrayal trauma or abandonment from our mother. Although we have been hurt, we may still yearn for her love but her behavior may cause us pain. We have to realize that her or their behavior may be the best they can give us at the time. We have to accept that however, we can implement boundaries to protect our peace and remain out of harm's way.

The Bible commands us to "seek peace and pursue it."[7] This doesn't only refer to peace with our fellow man but it also refers to peace within ourselves- inner peace. In this passage, Jesus is commanding us to pursue peace which requires action on our part. Daily we should do things that bring us to peace.

Particularly to combat hypervigilance, true self-care helps us to relax our nervous system so that we can maintain a calm state and reduce the impacts of anxiety. When we return to a calm baseline, we can enjoy happiness even when things around us are tense or overwhelming. Dr Maike Neuhaus, psychologist and founder of The Flourishing Doc states "Life circumstances play only a tiny role. A very large proportion of our happiness comes down to our daily actions. They start with the basics like having a healthy lifestyle, exercising, and getting a good amount of sleep."[8]

We have all heard about chemical imbalances in the brain and how they can result in mental health issues such as depression, anxiety, and schizophrenia. It has been scientifically proven that we can manipulate these same chemicals to improve our mood and restore happiness which produces a calm baseline. Research has proven that there are four brain chemicals that when released make us feel good and boost our mood—serotonin, dopamine, endorphins, and oxytocin. Low doses of many of these feel-good hormones are linked to depression, moodiness, and low motivation. Many of the activities that I'm about to introduce to you have been stigmatized and not embraced by our community. Regardless of the stigmas, these activities have healing powers that restore us from inherited trauma and hypervigilance.

Questions for Reflection

1. Jot down situations in which you were disappointed or hurt because you did not have boundaries in place.

Activity
Jot down 3 boundaries you will implement along with consequences for each.

Dopamine

Nijiama

Have you ever quit something when it felt difficult or lost the desire to finish a project? That feeling is possibly due to low dopamine. Known as the pleasure hormone, dopamine is a neurotransmitter. It is where much of our motivation derives from because it causes us to want to try things and repeat behavior.

Dopamine is in fact what makes addiction so luring as it is also released during sex and illicit drug use. Those cravings we have are because of the dopamine released from our brain. However, there are healthy and natural ways for our body to release the right amounts of dopamine.

Acts of kindness towards others, getting good sleep, eating favorite foods, taking vacations, and exercising are all means to encourage our body to release dopamine. Low levels of dopamine have been linked to moodiness, anxiety, and social anxiety. It's also responsible for a low libido. Diseases such as Parkinson's have been linked to dopamine deficits as well.[9]

Serotonin

Nijiama

Have you ever sat inside on a rainy day watching movies? Typically, this makes you feel very relaxed, drowsy, and groggy. Once you walk outside, your spirit is automatically lifted when the sun greets you. This euphoric feeling is the serotonin level increasing in your body. The sun rays hitting your face lifting your spirits while fighting off depression and anxiety.[10]

Now I know some of you may be reading this saying, "I was raised not to sit in the sun." Ughhh. This is one of those unhelpful ideals we brought over from slavery. As our ancestors toiled the fields daily under the iron fists of cruel slave owners, their skin darkened thus impacting their status on the plantation. Black enslaved people who were lighter in skin tone were allowed to work inside away from the burning sun to perform household chores while the darker-skinned slaves worked outside in the scorching heat. Because of this, our community has perceived the sun to be our enemy. This is indeed another example of what Dr. Joy DeGruy-Leary refers to as Post Traumatic Slave Syndrome or P.T.S.S.[11]

People with more melanin in their skin tend to be Vitamin D deficient and I am one of those people. We must learn to embrace spending time in the sun because it is helpful for us. Spending 10-15 outside in sunshine per day is one of the best methods of increasing serotonin levels and improving our moods.

Low serotonin levels, on the other hand, can cause one to feel anxious, irritable, depressed, fatigued, and exhausted.[10] The truth is, for a variety of reasons, our bodies need the sun.

Oxytocin

Nijiama

Oxytocin is referred to as the love hormone by Harvard Health. This hormone helps us to bond and connect with others. Oxytocin is the feeling we get when we are in love. Oxytocin is also released after birthing a new baby or receiving a warm hug.[13] **Yes,** this hormone can be released during sex but it can also be increased in much healthier ways. Studies have proven that singing in music groups, cuddling with a pet, and hugging can increase oxytocin. We don't have to chase sex to feel good.

Once or twice a month, I visit the spa to enjoy a pedicure. At the spa, I sip on warm tea or a glass of red wine while listening to my favorite R&B playlist. My feet are also massaged, moisturized, and rubbed. This experience soothes my soul and makes me feel like a baby being wrapped in a warm blanket after a cool bath. I can feel the calm washing over me and my nervous system being reset. This is peace.

GABA

Nijiama

I suffered a very unexpected mild heart attack. While I was in the hospital, almost every doctor and nurse recommended meditation to help reduce stress and anxiety. Meditation boosts the release of GABA. Gamma-aminobutyric acid, or GABA, is a neurotransmitter that puts us in a state of calm. It slows down our brain by blocking specific signals in the central nervous system which produces a calming effect. Faster brain waves, on the other hand, are believed to result in hypervigilance and stress. GABA provides us with a healthy response to stress by preventing neurons that send signals that fire up the body making us ready to pop off at any moment[14].

Perhaps you may be like me who did not know anyone in my community who mediated. My grandmother believed meditation was a tool of the devil. I just assumed it wasn't for me and ignored it.

After the heart attack, I began to research and practice meditation. Over time, I realized that I'd been practicing meditation without knowing it. For example, when I'm lying on the beach listening to the waves while taking deep breaths. The feeling of peace that falls upon me is GABA and Serotonin being released and putting me at ease.

Mediation isn't merely a strange ritual. It is backed by research and its results are proven. "It seems the longer you do meditation, the better your brain will be at self-regulation," said Bin He, a neuroengineer at Carnegie Mellon University, states. "You don't have to consume as much energy at rest and you can more easily get yourself into a more relaxed state[15]."

Studies have shown that regular meditation practice increases the release of GABA. A 2010 study by the Boston University School of Medicine found a 27% increase in GABA levels in patients after just 60 minutes of mindful meditation practice.[16]

If you were not raised with techniques to soothe yourself like I was, you can try some of the techniques we've mentioned. If your quest is for inner peace, targeting the right chemical releases in your brain is a great way to achieve that. These activities eliminate pain and trauma from our bodies and restore us to the natural state of peacefulness. Our brain is so powerful that we should be able to overcome almost any obstacle albeit sickness, disease, trauma, or heartbreak while maintaining an abundance of inner peace. Self-care, which is full body care, makes this possible.

Endorphins

Shamon

One of the highlights of my day is spending time in the gym. While strength training and performing cardio, I'm able to release the stress from the day while listening to my favorite playlists. The change to my body as well as the other benefits I gain from exercise help me to feel good about myself. Because endorphins are released to help the body cope with pain after a workout I begin to feel as if I'm unstoppable. Exercise is a true confidence and self-esteem booster.[12]

Activity
Simple meditation exercise:

- Sit or lie, in a cool space, in a posture that makes you comfortable yet still alert. Close your eyes or lower your gaze.
- Focus on relaxing. Take five deep breaths exhaling in and out.
- One by one, relax every area of your body starting with your toes and working your way up to your neck and head. As you work through the body, pay attention to how each part feels.
- If your mind begins to wander, gently redirect but do not judge or be harsh to yourself.
- Pay attention to how relaxed and calm you feel.
- Remain in this state of calm and relax as long as you can.
- You can focus on your favorite scripture or affirmation during this time as well.
- Do this as frequently as you can, trying to increase the time.

Chapter 13

Your Tribe is Your Vibe

"If You Want To Go Fast, Go Alone, And If You Want To Go Far, Go Together."
– **African Proverb**

Nijiama

Have you ever heard someone say any of the following:

- I can do bad all by myself
- I am solo dolo
- I don't need anyone
- I don't need friends– No new friends
- I don't trust women as friends

Perhaps you have said these things yourself. These are trauma responses, y'all. These statements reflect the thoughts and feelings embraced when we have been hurt, particularly when we have been rejected.

One of my favorite scenes from the movie *Poetic Justice* is when the main characters made a stop at the cookout.[17] Or more recently, I love the scene in the HBO/Max hit television show *Insecure* when Tasha invited Lawrence to the cookout.[18] In each of these scenes, they show family and friends eating, chatting, and laughing. This exemplifies the best of our culture. We enjoy coming together, with the aunties cooking our favorite side dishes while the Uncles serve up deliciousness on the grill. Per usual, a spades game occurs then we end the night with the latest line dance. This is an example of community.

In ancient West Africa, communities made up of extended families worked together to form villages.

Together they cultivated the land, raised children, and protected each other.[19] Here in the US, during the 40s, 50s, and 60s, Black families remained connected and lived together. They cared for children left orphaned on the streets, threw block parties during the summer, and hosted rent parties when someone could not pay their rent. Community is ingrained in our DNA. We are community-driven beings and thrive in a tribe.

This is one of the reasons the Bible encourages us to attend church by stating "to not forsake the assembling of the saints." Church is more than just a place to go on Sundays; it's about the community of people we get to interact with when we are there. The warm hugs we receive at church increase our oxytocin while the music lifts our spirits and the message empowers us.

As human beings, we are better in a community. Mental disorders such as depression and schizophrenia feed off of isolation. The key to doing community well, however, is that we must show up emotionally whole.

One of the things that hinders us from being in a community is feeling judged or criticized. I've been in many circles where people put on facades and lie about their backstories to cover up the truth. To them, they fear being judged if their peers knew they were once poor, raised in the hood, or in a single-parent home.

We are inclined to judge—we are human and that's how we are wired. We have to train ourselves, however, to judge up. This prevents us from looking down on others. It makes us open to hearing the stories of others through a lens of compassion and acceptance instead of ridicule and harsh criticism.

I had to train myself to judge-up when I worked in DC. I would hear many harrowing stories and I had to ask for God's help to guide me to see these individuals and families as He would see them. God suddenly began to show me all of my faults and mistakes.

As I was reading the Bible one day, I paid close attention to the passage that described Jesus meeting the women at the well. There, Jesus mentioned she had five husbands and was living in an unwed situation.[20] I noticed that Jesus didn't follow up with, "What's the matter with you, you can't keep a man?" He mentioned her past to let her know that He was fully aware of her history and current circumstances but it didn't matter to Him. All that mattered was the moment they were in at that time. To Jesus, this woman had worth and value and He had a conversation with her to let her know that. That is judging up.

There is also another benefit of living in a community and that is the role models we gain. I can recall being at a church event when a woman reacted harshly as one of the other women, Tracey, was collecting donations. When Tracey asked the woman if she was going to participate, she pounded her fist on the table, raised her voice, and stated that she didn't have the money and to stop asking her. It was an uncomfortable moment for sure. However, Tracey responded in a manner unlike any I had seen. Instead of becoming irate, she remained polite and said, "Oh ok" and moved on to the next person. I admired the level of self-control Tracey possessed (a calm baseline) and the power that was within her to not allow this woman to ruin her moment or the day. This situation happened almost twenty years ago, but I still carry it with me. It showed me the type of woman I wanted to be– one who is in total control of her emotions. This moment was pivotal for me because it was the catalyst for making inner changes. Tracey became one of many role models for me.

Role models are instrumental in helping us heal. There have been many people who modeled for me emotionally healthy womanhood and couples who showed me how to honor my marriage. I did not grow up with many examples of successful marriages around me yet I knew that's what I wanted. Living in a community has helped me to identify role models who teach me from a distance.

We also must keep people in our tribe who are different and think differently from us. This is how we grow and learn. Our brain searches for similarities and patterns. Similarities bring us comfort but they don't help us grow. This is why trauma bonding becomes so easy because the brokenness and toxic behavior inside of us attract the brokenness and toxic behavior inside of others.

Once we connect with people who are progressing in areas that we want to achieve, we change as our ideals change. Good role models provide us with a much-needed shift in thinking that produces greatness. TD Jakes stated, "Relationships are indicators. They are indicators of the currency of growth…. Your new friends ought to make your old

friends uncomfortable."[21] Ask yourself if your
friendships reflect the direction you want to head.

Questions for Reflection

1. List the people who make you feel at peace when you spend time with them.

2. List the people who you laugh with when you spend time with them.

3. List the people who give you honest feedback.

4. How can you be open to new friendships?

5. Is there anyone that you know who you are interested in building a friendship with? How can you initiate that?

6. How can you make sure your friendships remain healthy?

Activity
Do this with your friends. List 7 traits of a good friend. Compare your lists.

Chapter 14

For the Culture

"*If we are to preserve culture we must continue to create it*" by **Johan Huizinga**

Nijiama

As enslaved foreigners to this land, we lost quite a bit. We lost our African identity and culture. As we were forced to assimilate, we lost the appetite for certain foods we once enjoyed, the type of names we once were called, and how we lived our lives. For us to remain docile and compliant, slave owners condemned and criticized our food, dress, and language forcing us to release everything we knew about our homeland. Because we lost our collective identity, we tend to function, even today, out of an orphan spirit trying to determine who we are and what works for us. But some of the ideals we have embraced are not a fit for us and do more damage than good. Although we are not monolithic, we have to also understand how we are wired and what is good for the culture.

You have never met me but if I say to you, out of the blue any of these comments:

- What had happened was
- All my life I had to fight
- Black don't crack
- You ain't got no job, Tommy!
- She put her foot in it
- You reneged
- Who made the potato salad?
- Stay Woke

You will know exactly what I am referencing. These are statements that are significant to our culture. Being Black isn't simply limited to race it's a culture. We need to embrace it, be proud of it, protect it, and work hard to continue to improve it. Our world is made up of many beautiful cultures. Let's celebrate the one we are born into.

Black culture is power, fortitude, and resilience. With fierce determination, we have moved from being perceived as the least of the least in American society to being elected to the highest positions in the free world——we did that. However, we did it by doing something different.

I have a friend who grew up in Barry Farms, a neighborhood in SE Washington, DC. My friend dropped out of high school in the 11th grade. I asked her why she chose to drop out and she said, "That's what I saw. My cousins and everyone in my neighborhood dropped out so that's what I did too." Years later, her daughter graduated from high school and then earned her Bachelor's. She is now earning her Master's degree. Her daughter is the change agent– she did something different. She is changing the expression of the DNA in her family. That is powerful!

We owe it to ourselves to continue to break the bondages of slavery chain by chain and link by link for our families and that requires us each to do something different. When we do something different, we are reversing the generational curses. For as long as I've been working with people, I have seen with my own eyes families mutate from homeless addicts to college-educated professionals and from low-wage, illiterate workers to business owners. It all starts with doing something different-something that matters, something that will last.

Being catalysts for change requires us to go against what may have occurred in the past or even the traditions of our elders. Some family traditions need to be dismantled and those are the ones that cause us more harm than good; the ones we develop out of our hypervigilance.

Shamon and I wanted to build a healthy family and so we do things differently. In our marriage, "I get to love you" has become our mantra. This sets the tone for how we treat and respond to each other. So, we speak kindly to each other, apologize swiftly, and admit our wrongs. We serve each other and consider each other in every decision we make. This not only affects our marriage but it impacts our children. We are now able to model for our children an emotionally healthy relationship. They do not have to look to the media for guidance because they see it every day in their home.

We must also protect our culture and communities!

We protect these critical paradigms and spaces by continually assessing and improving upon the roles we occupy to make things better for all those within our physical reach and social influences. Therefore, if we are an educator at an inner city school or a predominantly Black charter school, we should do so with enthusiasm daily knowing that our children's lives as well as their futures are in our hands. If we are the leader of our church's children's choir, we should do so with passion and creativity, understanding that the next Whitney Houston could be in our midst. If we coach the basketball team, we should teach our children skills they can use on the court and in life. If we join the fraternity/sorority or 'it' social group, let's use our healed perspective and life tools to treat others in these groups better than the trauma we experienced or inflicted on others — if we're going to cancel something meaningful, let's cancel the mean girl behavior and harmful masculinity. If we have influential virtual platforms, let's use them to give perspective, tools, and takeaways that positively transform how people think and show up for themselves and others.

We protect our culture by honoring our work and businesses. We do so by avoiding fights at the new, Black-owned restaurant or lounge. We protect by not picking up a gun and killing each other. We protect by creating music and other forms of media that honor and celebrate our men, women, and culture. We protect by owning businesses that provide top-tier customer service and behave professionally. We protect by highlighting, complementing, and empowering Black excellence whenever we see or learn about it—whether it's at the mall, at the park, in the nail salon or barbershop, in the local news, or on social media.

Although we know our past in this country is traumatic, we should learn from it and continue to build on what we have accomplished instead of being concerned over what we do not have and comparing ourselves to other cultures. We can be fully aware that privilege exists without complaining about it. Most who are born with privilege will not acknowledge it because it means they have to put their privilege down at times. Instead of resenting their privilege, let's continue to build our own. This is one of the many reasons for networking, living in certain communities, attending church, and being members of certain social and professional groups. When these environments are healthy, they provide an array of opportunities to connect with like-minded individuals and these connections can produce results that we need to excel. Therefore, we too can make a quick phone call when little Johnny gets into trouble or contact grandfather to request a donation to start our business, or in the simplest form leave our full ethnic name on the resume without fretting that we will be denied the position. Yet, again we must become emotionally whole so that we can be the best versions of ourselves when we are in these spaces and know how to maintain these vital relationships healthily.

We want to leave you with this final note: Relationships are essential. However, the associates we meet, the friends we gain, and the loved ones we have will always give us a thousand reasons to cut them off, be angry with them, and harbor unforgiveness. They are flawed human beings– it is what it is. I'm quite sure that when our work on this earth is complete and we are on our deathbed inhaling our final breaths of air and our heart is beating its final beats, we will not declare, "I sure wish I had cursed out my neighbor," or "I wish I could use my last few heartbeats to argue with my ex-wife." I am however sure we will say something such as:

I wish I had more time to be a father to my son

I wish I could spend one more day laughing with my friends

I wish I had more time to provide wisdom to my daughter

I wish I could see the accomplishment of my goals

I wish I could hug my grandmother one more time

I wish I could have one more dinner with my sister

I wish I had spent more time loving myself

I wish I had just a bit more energy to leave something behind that matters, and that people will remember me for

Let's live in wholeness making every moment count so that when it's all over there will be no regrets. If trauma can be inherited so can love, wealth, and emotional wellness– change begins with us.

Now, Let The Weak Say I Am Strong

Emotionally Immature Behavior	Emotionally Whole Behavior
Avoids conflict	Addresses conflict directly and sees it as a powerful tool
Holds grudges	Forgives quickly
Screams, yells, curses, and fights	Controls temper, emotions, and feelings
Brags/Arrogance	Speaks highly of others/Enjoys quiet luxury
Blames others	Takes accountability
Allows others to walk over them, use them, and make them uncomfortable	Has boundaries and respects the boundaries of others
Speaks without thinking	Is mindful of how their words impact others
Plays the victim	Sees themselves as an overcomer
Holds on to old ways of thinking and doing things	Spends time with people who can help them embrace change and view life differently
Uses money, power, love, and other resources to get people to do what they want	Allows people to exercise their free will on their own accord

Questions for Reflection

1. Now that you have read this book, list 3 new things you will implement.

2. List 3 things you have learned about yourself during this reading.

3. List any "Aha moments" or additional insight you may have gained in general from reading this.

Activity
Discuss or share this book with 5 people you know. Let's continue to spread healing.

Notes & Citations

Chapter 2

1. Gallen, J. (Director). (2023). *Selective Outrage* [Film]. Netflix Studios.
2. Valeii, K. (4 Sept, 2022). *How does intergenerational trauma work?* Verywell Health https://www.verywellhealth.com/intergenerational-trauma-5191638
3. *PBS.* (2015, July 15). *Jim Crow and Plessy Vs Ferguson Slavery By Another Name.* https://www.pbs.org/tpt/slavery-by-another-name/themes/jim-crow/
4. Logan, R. (2019, May 11). *I remember that day.* NEA Today. https://www.nea.org/nea-today/all-news-articles/i-remember-day
5. Semuels, A. (2015, July 30). *White flight never ended.* The Atlantic https://www.theatlantic.com/business/archive/2015/07/white-flight-alive-and-well/399980/
6. Gorey, J. (2020, Aug 15). *How white flight segregated American cities and suburbs.* Apartment Therapy. https://www.apartmenttherapy.com/white-flight-2-36805862
7. Redlining Jackson C. (2021, Aug. 17). *What is redlining?* New York Times. https://www.nytimes.com/2021/08/17/realestate/whatisredlining.html#:~:text=The%20term%20has%20come%20to,were%20therefore%20deemed%20risky%20investments.

8. Plumer, B. (2020, Aug 24). How decades of racist housing policy left neighborhoods sweltering. New York Times. https://www.nytimes.com/interactive/2020/08/24/climate/racism-redlining-cities-global-warming.html

9. Kizilhan, J et al. (2021 Dec 22). *Transgenerational transmission of trauma across three Generations of Alevi Kurds*. National Library of Medicine. https://www.nytimes.com/interactive/2020/08/24/climate/racism-redlining-cities-global-warming.html

10. Sandman C. (2011, Nov. 9). *Change in mother's mental state can influence her baby's development before and after birth*. Association for Psychological Science.https://www.psychologicalscience.org/news/releases/a-fetus-can-sense-moms-psychological-state.html

11. Developmental Science. (2018, Oct.8). *Can a pregnant woman's experience influence her baby's temperament*? Development Science. https://www.developmentalscience.com/blog/2018/10/1/can-a-pregnant-womans-experience-influence-her-babys-temperament#:~:text=Also%2C%20pregnant%20women's%20high%20levels,disease%2C%20cognitive%20problems%2C%20and%20stress

Chapter 3

1. Brennan D, MD. (25 October 2021). *What is hypervigilance.*Web MD https://www.webmd.com/mental-health/what-is-hypervigilance

2. Brewer L, (2013, Aug 13). *Hyper-Vigilance' about race linked to elevated blood pressure in black patients*. Johns Hopkins Medical. https://www.hopkinsmedicine.org/news/media/releases/hyper_vigilance_about_race_linked_to_elevated_blood_pressure_in_black_patients

Chapter 4

1. US Department of Labor. (2011 May). https://www.dol.gov/sites/dolgov/files/WHD/legacy/files/FairLaborStandAct.pdf

2. Austin, A. Economic Policy Institute (2013, June 18). *The unfinished march.* https://www.epi.org/publication/unfinished-march-overview/

3. Kendi, I. (2016 May 27). The 11 most racist US presidents. Huffington Post. Black Voices https://www.huffpost.com/entry/would-a-president-trump-m_b_10135836?utm_campaign=share_email&ncid=other_email_o63gt2jcad4

4. NAACP Legal Defense Fund. The Case that Changed America, Brown Vs Board of Education.https://www.naacpldf.org/brown-vs-board/southern-manifesto-massive-resistance-brown/#:~:text=On%20February%2025%2C%201956%2C%20Senator,forestall%20and%20prevent%20school%20integration.

Momma Trauma

1. Weinberger E (writer), & Jamal-Warner M, (Director). *The Cosby Show.* (1990, April 5). Season 6 Ep 23. [Tv series episode].

2. Larnell, M. (2028). *Roxanne Roxanne* (Film), Netflix.

3. Equal Justice Initiative. (2018, Jan. 1). *Black Families Severed by Slavery.* https://eji.org/news/history-racial-injustice-Black-families-severed-by-slavery/#:~:text=Roughly%20half%20of%20all%20enslaved,of%20Black%20boys%20and%20girls.

4. Brennan D, MD. (25 October 2021). *What is hypervigilance.*Web MD https://www.webmd.com/mental-health/what-is-hypervigilance

Poppa was a Rolling Stone

1. Van Veen. D. (11 July 2019). *The value of a good father.* AG News. https://news.ag.org/en/articles/news/2019/06/the%20value%20of%20a%20good%20father

2. Children's Bureau. (12 May 2023). *A Father's Impact on Child Development.* https://www.all4kids.org/news/blog/a-fathers-impact-on-child-development

3. Gordon, B Phd (2014, Feb. 4). *Hooked on messy loving.* Psychology Today. https://www.psychologytoday.com/us/blog/obesely-speaking/201402/hooked-messy-loving#:~:text=You%20may%20have%20been%20born,the%20destructive%20consequences%20of%20addiction.

The Wounds of Masculinity

1. Ferenik, J.(2019, Dec. 11) bell hooks and masculinity. Medium https://jakubferencik.medium.com/bell-hooks-toxic-masculinity-adf46cdc6d11

Chapter 5

1. National Drug Intelligence Center. (Jan. 2001). *Illinois drug threat assessment.* https://www.justice.gov/archive/ndic/pubs/652/cocaine.htm

2. Marriotte, M. (1989, Feb. 20). *After 3 years, crack plague In new york only gets worse.*

    New York Times. https://www.nytimes.com/1989/02/20/nyregion/after-3-years-crack-plague-in-new-york-only-gets-worse.html

3. Lejuez, C. et al. (2011 Sep 28). Risk Factors in the Relationship between Gender and Crack/Cocaine. National Library of Medicine.

    https://www.ncbi.nlm.nih.gov/pmc/articles/PMC3182264/

Chapter 7

1. Mathis, T. (2023 Sept. 22). *What a prisoner can teach you about financial security.* Forbes.
   https://www.forbes.com/sites/forbesbooksauthors/2023/09/22/what-a-prisoner-at-san-quentin-prison-can-teach-you-about-financial-security/?sh=3d521eb5495c
2. NPR (2019 Dec. 20). *Curtis Carroll: What can you learn about life when you have a life sentence.*

   https://www.npr.org/2019/12/20/789744339/curtis-carroll-what-can-you-learn-about-life-when-you-have-a-life-sentence

3. Munroe Globa*l*. (2020 Nov. 5). *Understanding the purpose for Your life.* Dr. Myles Munroe.
   https://www.youtube.com/watch?v=gTgcGlnK1kk

4. Obama M. (2022). *The Light We Carry.* Crown Publishing.

Chapter 8

1. Smalls, N (2021) [Unpublished raw data mon Emotional Health]. The black girl's guide to healing emotional wounds.
2. Conversations with Today's Black Father, Research Interview. Sept. 2020.
3. All Nations Chicago. (2021, Oct 26). Group Therapy. [Video].https://www.youtube.com/watch?v=XTj-yL7NKDk&t=901s
4. Creed (2000). With Arms Wide Open. *Human Clay.* Wind-up
5. Maroon 5 (2002) She will be loved. Songs About Jane. Octone.
6. GIACOMAZZO B. (9 March 2022). *Afrotech 25 Years After The Notorious B.I.G.'s Passing, Here's How His Children Are Carrying On His $160M Legacy.* Afrotech. https://afrotech.com/biggie-smalls-notorious-b-i-g-children-net-worth

7.Harris, I. (2022) B.I.G. *called himself 'black And ugly As ever,' however, he spit sex lyrics And maintained A strong female fanbase.* Madamenoire.
https://madamenoire.com/1309909/the-women-who-loved-notorious-big/

8.The Notorious BIG (1995). *One More Chance, Remix.* Bad Boy.
9.Foxy Brown (1996). Ill Na Na. *Foxy Brown.* Def Jam.
10.Rihanna (2017) Sex with Me. Anti. RocNation
11.Cardi B and Megan Thee Stallion. (2022) WAP. Atlantic.
12.Hodgekiss A. (2016 Jan 6). *The Science of sex: Why love hurts, sex helps us live longer and kissing is good for health*
https://www.standardmedia.co.ke/entertainment/news/article/2000187173/the-science-of-sex-why-love-hurts-sex-helps-us-live-longer-and-kissing-is-good-for-health
13. Star, D. (1998). Sex and the City, HBO.
14.Wilcox, B. (2021 Dec 1). *Two is healthier than one.* Institute for Family Studies. https://ifstudies.org/blog/two-is-wealthier-than-one-marital-status-and-wealth-outcomes-among-preretirement-adults-
15.NIV version *The Holy Bible.* 2001. (Song of Solomon 4:16)

Chapter 7

1. Van der Kolk, B. MD. (2015). *The Body Keeps the Score.* Penguin Books
2. Smalls, N (2021) [Unpublished raw data mon Emotional Health]. the black girl's guide to healing emotional wounds.

Chapter 9

1. Braverman J. (13 May 2020). *Love & Hip Hop' reality TV show star charged with fraud of coronavirus relief loan.* 11 alive.com
https://www.11alive.com/article/news/crime/maurice-fayne-arkansas-mo-charged-fraud-coronavirus-loan/85-5f315d7c-43d6-401c-8b97-f25648d9eb18

2. Elison, J. Fact of Life (Aug 1979). NBC

Collins L. (18 June 2021). *What research says about two-parent families keeping kids out of jail and in school.* Deseret News. https://www.deseret.com/2021/6/17/22538277/what-research-says-about-two-parent-families-keeping-kids-out-of-jail-brookings-aei-family-studies#:~:text=Among%20study%20highlights%3A,more%20likely%20to%20be%20poor.

3. NPR (2019 Dec. 20). *Curtis Carroll: what can you learn about life when you have a life sentence.* https://www.npr.org/2019/12/20/789744339/curtis-carroll-what-can-you-learn-about-life-when-you-have-a-life-sentence

Chapter 10

1.Meador, J. (2023 July 29). *The Misunderstood Reason Millions of Americans Stopped Going to Church,* The Atlantic. https://www.theatlantic.com/ideas/archive/2023/07/christian-church-communitiy-participation-drop/674843/

2. NIV version *The Holy Bible.* 2001.

3. PBS. (2010, October, 11). G*od in America.* https://www.pbs.org/wgbh/americanexperience/films/godinamerica/

4. NMAAHC (2023 Aug 21). *Nat Turner's Rebellion.* https://nmaahc.tumblr.com/post/127260651340/nat-turners-rebellion

5. Brown D. (2021 Jan 6). *Ebenezer Baptist: MLK's church makes new history with Warnock victory.* The Washington Post. https://www.washingtonpost.com/history/2021/01/03/ebenezer-baptist-king-mlk-warnoc

6. Pien D. (11 Feb 2010). *Black Panther's Party Free Breakfast Program.* Blackpast. https://www.Blackpast.org/african-american-history/Black-panther-partys-free-breakfast-program-1969-1980/

7.Civil Rights Movement Archive. *Freedom Now.* https://www.crmvet.org/tim/tim63b.htm#:~:text=He's%20known

%20as%20the%20%22fighting,methods%20of%20education%2
0for%20Black

Chapter 12

1. Cambridge Dictionary.
   https://dictionary.cambridge.org/us/dictionary/english/tr
   iggered
2. Van der Kolk, B. MD. (2015). *The Body Keeps the
   Score* Penguin Books
3. Leave it to Beaver. (1957). Republic Studios.
4. Father's Day; A Kirk Franklin Story. (2023 Sept.)
   https://www.youtube.com/watch?v=49SCqvyZM7Q,
5. Winfrey, O. 60 Minutes, Relationships
6. https://www.medicalnewstoday.com/articles/145855
7. NIV The Holy Bible 2001
8. https://www.theflourishingdoc.com/
9. Watson, S. (2021, July 20). *Dopamine; the pathway to
   pleasure.* Harvard Health
   Publishing.https://www.health.harvard.edu/mind-and-
   mood/dopamine-the-pathway-to-pleasure
10. Healthline. (2023 April 17). *Everything you need to
    know about serotonin.*
    https://www.healthline.com/health/mental-
    health/serotonin
11. De Gruy J. (2017). *Post Traumatic Slave Syndrome.*
    (Sept. 11, 2017) Joy Degruy Publications Inc.
12. Cleveland Clinic. *Endorphins.* (2022 May
    19). https://my.clevelandclinic.org/health/body/23040-
    endorphins
13. Harvard Health Publishing, *Oxytocin the love hormone.*
    (13 June 2023) https://www.health.harvard.edu/mind-
    and-mood/oxytocin-the-love-hormone
14. Cleveland Clinic. *Gamma-aminobutyric acid (GABA).*
    (2022 April 25).
    https://my.clevelandclinic.org/health/articles/22857-
    gamma-aminobutyric-acid-gaba
15. Sukul K, (19 April 2019). *Understanding the power of
    meditation.* Brainfacts.org.
    https://www.brainfacts.org/thinking-sensing-and-

behaving/thinking-and-awareness/2019/understanding-the-power-of-meditation-041919

16. Streeter C, et al (2007 May 13). *Yoga Asana sessions increase brain GABA levels: a pilot study.* National Library of Medicine. https://pubmed.ncbi.nlm.nih.gov/17532734/

17. Singleton J. (Director). *Poetic Justice* [Film]. Columbia Pictures

18. Rae, I. (Director).(July 30 2017). (Season 2 Episode 2). [Insecure] HBO

19. Brewamate; A Bold Blend of News and Ideas. Early Societies in West Africa, 500-1600 CE (21 May 2021). https://brewminate.com/early-societies-in-west-africa-500-1600-ce/

20. NIV version *The Holy Bible.* 2001. (Song of Solomon 4:16)

21. Jakes, T (2023). *Provoked to Purpose.* https://sermons.love/td-jakes/14543-td-jakes-provoked-to-purpose.html

Books Written by Nijiama Smalls

The Black Girl's Guide to Healing Emotional Wounds
The Black Girl's Guide to Healing Emotional Wounds -Devotional
The Black Girl's Guide to Healing Emotional Wounds- Journal

For more information about Nijiama and Shamon, visit the website: nijiamasmalls.com

For emotional health and healing resources visit the website:
Theblackgirlsguidetohealingemotionalwounds.com

Connect with us on a daily basis:
Facebook: Shamon and Nijiama
IG: @nijiamasmallsinreallife
        @shamonsmalls
        @theblackgirlsguidetohealing
TikTok: @nijiamasmalls